Two Views of the South-West Africa Campaign 1914-15

Two Views of the South-West Africa Campaign 1914-15

With Botha in the Field
Recollections of Botha's Bodyguard Troop
Moore Ritchie

With Botha's Army in the
Imperial Light Horse

J. P. Kay Robinson

LEONAUR

Two Views of the South-West Africa Campaign 1914-15
With Botha in the Field Recollections of Botha's Bodyguard troop
by Moore Ritchie
and
With Botha's Army in the Imperial Light Horse
by J. P. Kay Robinson

First published under the titles
With Botha in the Field
and
With Botha's Army

FIRST EDITION

Leonaur is an imprint
of Oakpast Ltd

ISBN: 978-1-78282-237-0 (hardcover)
ISBN: 978-1-78282-238-7 (softcover)

http://www.leonaur.com

Contents

With Botha in the Field Recollections of Botha's
Bodyguard Troop   7

With Botha's Army in the Imperial Light Horse   103

With Botha in the Field Recollections of Botha's Bodyguard Troop

The Author

Contents

Foreword 13

Kemp and Beyers 15

De Wet 19

Kemp's Escape 23

Fourie 28

The Preliminary Canter 34

The First Trek Into the Namib Desert 48

The Record Trek to Windhuk 57

The Last Phase 79

Appendix 92

J.B.
LIEUTENANT, HIS MAJESTY'S IMPERIAL FORCES,
IF THIS SHOULD CATCH THE EYE OF:
CHER AMI,—TO YOU:
IN MEMORY OF DAYS.
YOURS,
M. R.

Diagram of Campaign

Foreword

The ungentle reader (upon whom a malediction) will discover that this little book is not by any means exhaustive. But the gentle reader may find it to be what I hope it is. For him I wrote it.

Europe at the present time is lacerated in the greatest war of which man has knowledge. Compared with the doings in the Eastern and Western Fronts, in the Austro-Italian Theatre, or in the Dardanelles, the campaign of South Africa must take a modest place.

My idea is simply to make clear to the public (for example, all names I mention will be easily found on my diagrams, drawn from a German fully detailed map, the best of the South-West African Protectorate in existence) of gentle and patriotic readers something of the latter-day work of a gentleman and a patriot, justly famed amongst peoples with whom integrity and honour are still esteemed sovereign virtues.

"The Nonggai,"
Pretoria, S. Africa,
August 1915.

THE ONLY PHOTO OF THE MEETING OF GENERAL BOTHA AND
GENERAL SMUTS IN THE FIELD JUST BEFORE WINDHUK WAS
TAKEN

SECTION 1

Kemp and Beyers

Six weeks after the war-cloud smashed over Europe a man called on me. He was an old friend; but the point about him is that at that particular time I fancied him on his farm at least a thousand miles away.

"Hello!" I said in surprise. "Why this sudden appearance?"

"This is going to be a big thing, my boy. I am off 'Home.' They will need us all."

It impressed me. He was a person calm and methodical minded, and, like so many good men, he has been dead now many months. His words, which have proved true, were the first to turn my mind definitely to war-thoughts. Besides, the man whose trade is writing has always, when events are stirring, the itch to go, look and note.

In the branch of the Union Service to which I belong—the South African Police—none but reservists could then proceed to Europe; but when General Botha announced that he himself would take command of the Expeditionary Force to German South-West Africa, a bodyguard from the South African Police was decided upon, volunteers came forward, and on this unit I had the honour to serve.

The intention of the Union Authorities was to push forward with the German West Campaign as quickly as possible. The rebellion delayed operations roughly some three months—a period during which some exceedingly severe marchings and stiff rifle actions took place. I mention this deliberately, for in the stir of well-won applause following the victorious end of the campaign proper, the preliminary canter of the rebellion is perhaps somewhat forgotten.

It does not seem, in the light of later information, strictly true to say that the rebellion of 1914 broke upon the Union of South Africa

15

General Botha's Bodyguard leaving for the Front

in a manner wholly unexpected. But its ultimate development and extent did cause both surprise and great uneasiness. The details of its various activities over the country are by this time stale history. Leaving comment of a political nature alone, I confine myself briefly to the movements which, performed by General Botha and the loyalist troops, were so swift and accurate in their workings that they broke the back of the main risings before more than local disorganisation and the least possible amount of bloodshed had been achieved.

On the 12th of October the bodyguard for the German South-West Campaign assembled for field practices, etc., at Pretoria. On the 20th we heard that we should be leaving at an hour's notice, presumably for the South-West. The following day wild and disquieting rumours began to circulate from early morning. Maritz had gone into rebellion. Motorcars sped all forenoon between General Botha's house close to us and the Union Defence Headquarters. Our camp was full of alarms. The police of Pretoria became suddenly twice as many about the streets. Towards evening it was positively stated that plots were afoot aiming at nothing less than the life of General Botha; and the Main Guard, which had been mounted at the general's house from the day of the bodyguard's formation, was doubled. Not a soul was allowed within or around the modest grounds of the house without challenge at the point of the bayonet and presentment of the countersign. It will be long before memory loses the picture of those evenings, when through the lighted windows of the left wing of the house the Main Guard first and second reliefs got a view of a familiar ample figure in anxious consultations at a table upon which the electric light cast a mellow glow.

The next day, the 22nd of October, rumour gave way to fact. Rebellion had definitely broken out in the Transvaal and the Free State; Beyers, the ex-Commandant General, Kemp and others were leading in the Transvaal; the names of De Wet and Wessel Wessels were coupled with the Free State. For the second time within a year unhappy South Africa heard rumours of imminent Martial Law proclamations.

Monday morning, the 26th, arrived and found us still waiting; then the Bodyguard got twenty minutes' notice and entrained, horses, kits and everything for Rustenburg. We arrived there at five o'clock the following morning, and started at once in pursuit of rebel commandos which were led by Kemp and Beyers. Before starting, General Botha over a cup of coffee had an anxious consultation with his loyal commandants who had arrived to meet him. Throughout the day we trekked, with one brief halt only, and "outspanned" that night near Oliphant's Nek. During the day the loyal commandos located the rebels without much difficulty; they were routed in all directions, and some eighty were captured. At two o'clock in the morning we continued the trek, stopped in the forenoon on the railway line at Derby (close to Drakfontein, the scene of the British disaster to Benson's Horse during the South African War), and pushing on in the evening to Koster, learnt from incoming scouts that Kemp had escaped capture by minutes only. The direction of his flight was questionable at the time.

Returning to Pretoria, we remained there for a few days. The whole town was in a state of remarkable tension. The police were armed. Armed volunteers were called for. Loyalists were training after working hours in batches on various open spaces. It was freely whispered that the German South-West Campaign would be given up, so formidable was the threatened opposition to it. . . . I am writing this much less than a year later: and Windhuk has fallen, the Germans have surrendered their territory, and thousands of *burghers* and volunteers are returning to their homes.

On the 2nd of November we left Pretoria again. More trouble was brewing at Brits, close to Pretoria. We trekked straightway to Zoutpan's Drift, the commandos again pursuing a body of rebels who, cutting through the railway line, had caused damage at De Wilts or Greyling's Post, twenty miles or so outside the Union capital. Quite unwilling to make a stand, the insurgents were again put to flight, and General Botha returned to Pretoria the following day. In the meantime other loyalist columns in the Transvaal had taken to the field, and the rebellion seemed well in hand.

SECTION 2

De Wet

Compared with the Free State insurrection, the Transvaal affair appeared in many ways to be a small business from our point of view. In actuality it was nothing of the kind. It was, if anything, much more ugly in spirit. The genius of the Free State section of insurgents displayed itself chiefly in a highly finished exposition of lying, looting and "legging it."

De Wet's delirious harangue had not exhausted its nine-days' life as a masterpiece of unconscious humour when General Botha left Pretoria for the Free State on November 9. Again, I am not concerned with the highly complex motives which prompted the veteran Dutch General to make his delightful "Five Bob Outrage" speech and other things at Vrede. Flogging dead horses is a useless job, anyway.

During the journey to the Free State, our guard on the train was extremely strict. Though every possible precaution of secrecy had been taken, we were positively told to be prepared to find the train fired upon. But, if during such journeys preparedness was doubtless essential in the circumstances, it always seemed to me that we, or any one so placed, were pretty powerless to avert disaster should a properly directed shot from the darkness find its mark.

On November 11 we detrained at Theunissen, in the Free State. It was speedily clear that this part of the world was in the grip of disturbance. Telegraph poles all along the line had been wrecked; an amount of mild pillaging had been going on. The people of Theunissen were almost in panic. The two fights—one against Conroy, at Allaman's Kraal, the other and larger, against De Wet, at Doornberg—had been enormously magnified. General Botha was welcomed in genuine relief. We remained at arms in the train during the first part of the night. At 2 a.m. we were roused, and in less than half an hour were on the way across country to Winburg.

The arrival at the little railhead *dorp* of Winburg was remarkable. Scarcely were we halted and hand put to loosen girth before the loyalist leaders came running out in the morning sunshine to meet us. De Wet had left the place two hours before, disappearing with his following over the first *kopje*. He had caused absolute panic. His forces had cut the inhabitants off from all touch with the outer world. De Wet had commandeered all food supplies worth having. Houses had been looted and speeches were made in the marketplace. His followers had assured the people that the Empire was tottering, Germany had defeated Britain on land and sea, a hundred thousand were marching on Pretoria, and that Botha and his government were defeated and disgraced. And these statements were to a large extent believed.

It was but natural. Cut off the wire and rail communication of a South African *veld* town and you have isolation in the most thorough sense. In such a place at such a time mere statement may seem quite possibly the truth.

Towards evening we got news of the rebels, and a night-march was ordered. As we left the town the loyal people lined the streets, the fellows in the columns whistled "Tipperary," and we got a rousing farewell.

General Botha is celebrated amongst fighting men for many things, and his night-marching is one of them. He appears to believe to the fullest extent in night-marching. He had located De Wet at a place called Mushroom Valley, and parts of the commander-in-chief's forces had been sent to make a surrounding movement. During the all-night trek from Winburg to Mushroom Valley I had a first thorough experience of the true horrors of sleep-fighting. It was bitterly cold—cold as the Free State night on the *veld* knows how to be. And we could not smoke, could not talk above a faint murmur, and nodded in our saddles. The clear stars danced fantastically in the sky ahead of us, and the ground seemed to be falling away from us into vast hollows, then rising to our horses' noses ready to smash into us like an impalpable wall. After midnight, outspanning in a piercing wind, we formed square; main guard was posted over the general's car, and those lucky enough to escape turn of duty huddled together under cloaks and dozed fitfully until two-thirty.

From two-thirty till sunrise we trekked on. Suddenly, just after good daylight, the staff halted the column, glasses were put up, and away we swung half right into the *veld*. Up came the artillery and

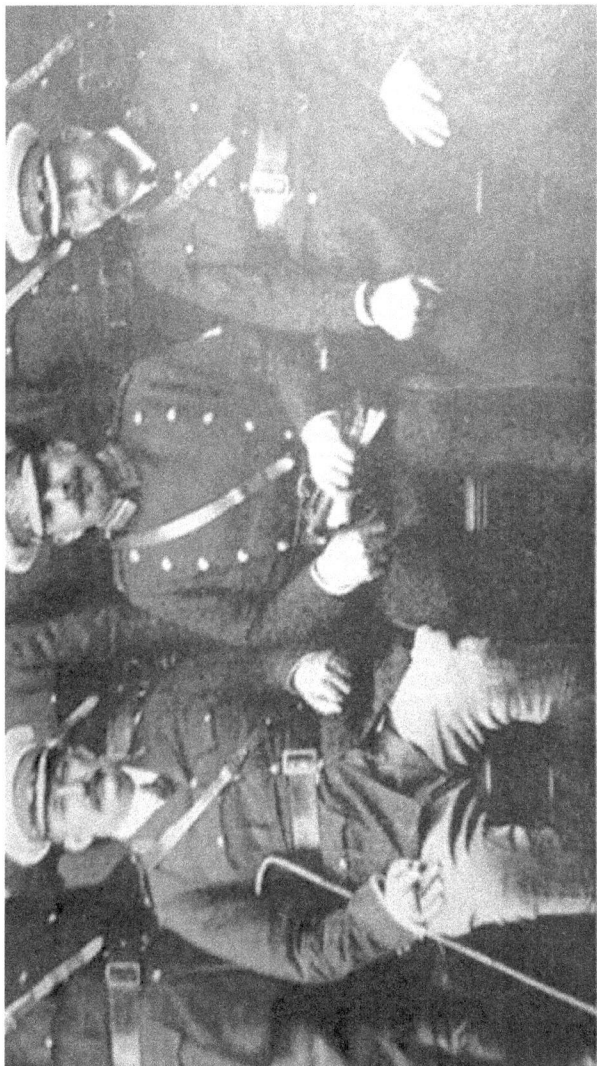

KEMP.   EVANS.   MAJOR BRANDT.

GROUP OF REBEL LEADERS

opened fire on a cluster of ant-sized figures four thousand yards ahead beneath the shoulder of a *kopje*. Had the thing not contained the very germ of tragedy it would have been laughable to see the way those figures scattered over the red *veld*. It was De Wet's commandos caught napping. Just before the shell fire our *burghers* had gone out ahead hell-for-leather on either flank. The whole column then advanced. After two hours' pretty hot work the action was over. We lost six killed against the rebels' twenty-two, and with twenty wounded on our side the rebel losses were proportionate. We took upwards of three hundred prisoners, De Wet himself escaping by the merest fluke. He lost all his transport, and generally ceased after the action to be a serious menace.

During the operations against De Wet I watched, when possible, the demeanour of the quiet South African patriot with whom fate had placed me in the field. I had last seen him many years before, gravely bowing from under a silk hat to a crowd that swayed and cheered as he drove through the streets of Manchester. And now duty found him in the field against an old comrade-in-arms. There was a sadness, there was a profound pathos about it. No wonder if to me it seemed that General Botha looked downcast indeed, if stern as well, during the rebellion. Life, surely, was not dealing too fairly by him.

Following Mushroom Valley, we trekked, with two brief outspans only, to Clocolan, all the time scattering De Wet's followers. At Clocolan we paused for one day, entrained men and horses and reached Kimberley, *via* Bloemfontein, on the 18th of November. The following day rebel activities were reported in the direction of Bloemhof; but after an eventless journey we returned to Kimberley on the 21st.

Kemp's Escape

It was at Kimberley that news came through that Kemp was making a desperate cross-country trek to get into German territory in the Upington neighbourhood. A reference to a map will show that Upington, on the Orange River, is on the extreme western borders of the Union; and it must be said that the trek which Kemp and the remnant of his moderate force, poorly mounted and equipped, had made since being routed by General Botha on the 27th of October (a month before) stands as a remarkable piece of work. We pushed on to Prieska, *via* De Aar, and reached Upington, on the scarcely completed new line from Prieska, on the 25th of November. The journey over the desert stretch from Prieska to Upington was full of alarms; during the night the train halted in the lonely *veld* owing to a washaway, and we stood to arms, throwing out cossack-posts around the train wherein the commander-in-chief slept. It was tremendously exciting work.

The old town of Upington was transformed in those days. Around the Dutch Reformed Church, standing peaceful and dazzling white in the torrid sun, were tents, wagons, horses, motorcars, signalling-parties, despatch-riders and infantry. Away over the hard red sand dunes to the north was the action zone, and from that direction every five minutes came sweating motor despatch-riders, who tore along to Headquarters. The following day news came through that the Imperial Light Horse and the Natal Carbineers had been engaging Kemp before and since dawn; almost cornered, he was making a final dash for the border to get into German South-West. It was an anxious time; each minute brought a fresh rumour as to the fighting and the thousands of men Kemp had got together for his desperate move. Our staff returned before dark, reporting an eventless day, with intermittent fighting.

On the 28th the staff went out in motors as far as Rooidam. They returned with bad news in the early afternoon. After a prolonged rear-guard action Kemp had succeeded, taking over to the Germans with him a force which was said to be far greater than had been supposed. (Need I add that after events showed there had been gross exaggeration?)

I offer, with reserve, the following ingenious explanation of Kemp's escape; it was told me later by several who saw the action. Near the end of his terrific trek through from the North-Western Transvaal to the German outpost for which he was making, Kemp was hotly pursued by the loyalist troops. His men were exhausted. Half of them were dismounted. All his horses were spent. In these conditions he was forced to the most trying form of fight—the rearguard and flank action. With his goal practically right ahead, he reached three of the parallel large sand dunes with which the *veld* around Upington is scattered. They were on his left flank. He swerved into them. Hotly pursued, he crossed two, and under the lee of the second left a party of good shots. Then, cantering away over the third, he doubled round on his tracks and with his exhausted followers made for the German outpost. When the Union troops came up they were ambushed at short range, and the check they got just served the fleeing rebel. In the pursuit afterwards our parties found traces of buried rations for horses and men. These had been provided with German thoroughness.

The second phase of the Free State Rebellion was a pantomime more than anything else; a week's pantomime acted in the open *veld* in rain that never stopped. It was the most miserable week I have known. We left Upington on the 29th of November, reaching Kroonstad, Orange Free State, late next evening. Here the commander-in-chief was met by General Smuts, Minister for Defence; a consultation took place, and as a result we left by train for Bethlehem in the evening. Our arrival was timely, too. The place was in a perfect uproar. Nobody knew what was going to happen next.

All the loyalist civilians were under arms. The large mill of the Kaffrarian Steam Flour Company had been converted into a fort which was, in case of necessity, impregnable to rifle-fire. The rebels in the field had declared the New Republic practically established, with temporary capital at Reitz. Just before we saddled up to track them the news came of De Wet's capture on the Malopi River, near Mafeking. The news put everyone in fresher spirits. The charm around the famous guerilla fighter had broken. That the Rebellion was doomed we all knew. But most of us were weary, nevertheless. It furnished a

THE LAST PURSUIT OF KEMP. FLYING COLUMN CROSSING THE ORANGE RIVER AFTER HIM

refresher.

We left a happier Bethlehem at a rainy dawn the next day. Half way to Reitz we outspanned in the rain. It rained all night. The following morning came back to mind a talk an old soldier and I had once while freezing one early morning awaiting the Channel boat at Greenock. Alluding to cold and misery, he said: "You don't know what it is, my son, till you've been held up for three nights by rain in war-time in the South African *veld*, and spent the time standing in water. I did it outside Mafeking." Well, I understand a little now.

The next day our scouts entered Reitz; the rebels had fled. For two days we operated against them. A day later General Botha returned to Reitz. Nothing was said at the time. The fact was that before we entrained at Reitz, on the 7th of December, Wessel Wessels and Serfontein were surrounded. A day later they surrendered: the Orange Free State Rebellion, in all its futility, was over.

TROOPS RETURNING TO PRETORIA AFTER NOOITGEDACHT. DECEMBER 16, 1914

Section 4

Fourie

Just before and during the commander-in-chief's long trek, other bodies of loyalist troops had been engaging the rebels. The most notable of these actions were against Muller at Bronkhorst Spruit (5th November, 1914; casualties, one killed and three wounded), and against Fourie at Hamanskraal (22nd November, 1914; casualties, three killed and ten wounded). Both these actions took place in the neighbourhood of Pretoria. As a result of them and the death of Beyers in the Vaal River, the rebellion in the Transvaal was virtually smashed. There remained only Fourie to be dealt with.

Fourie, late Major in the South African Defence Force, possibly the most fanatical of all the rebels, appears to have been a man of character and proved courage. Having got away at the action at Hamanskraal, he and his younger brother were moving about in the *veld* with ex-Major Pienaar and a moderate force. Their fantastic purpose was said to be the taking of Pretoria itself on Dingaan's Day, the 16th of December. As all the South African world knows, this date marks the anniversary of the famous fight of the Voortrekkers at Blood River in 1838. The day before a force of South African Police, Defence Force, and South African Mounted Riflemen left Pretoria, detrained at Greyling's Post, on the Pietersburg Line, and started in pursuit of the last big rebel commando at large. In this move we of the Bodyguard found ourselves acting; General Botha, who had returned to Pretoria after his severe field work, had gone to his farm for a few days' rest before the South-West campaign.

We trekked at dawn and during the whole of the following day, with one rain-sodden halt, till four in the afternoon. The rebels had doubled in their tracks after reaching a large dam at Blaaubank. Late in the afternoon our scouts returned to the column and reported having

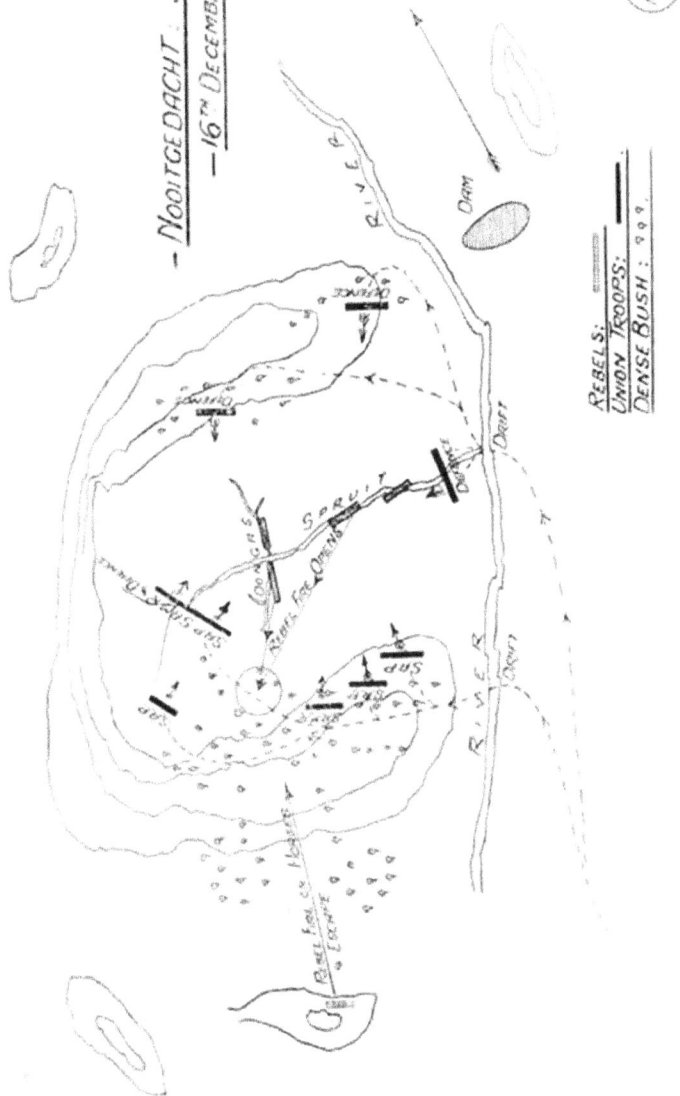

Diagram of Nooitgedacht

located the enemy three miles ahead, entrenched in a *donga*, or dried-up stony river course, on the farm Nooitgedacht No. 4. We prepared for action, and encountered the rebels in the next half hour. This, the first true action I had been in, was an extremely dirty affair; a man who had gone through some of the worst fights in the South African War afterwards assured me it was the hottest corner he had ever been in. Bush-country fighting is detestable chiefly because you cannot see your enemy until you are on top of him. Our centre cantered in extended order up an avenue flanked by dense bush. We were laughing and asking where the deuce the rebels were, when a hail of rifle fire at short range greeted us. Our fellows were out of their saddles in a second, and advanced to the attack through the bush. Meantime, the South African Police extreme left had swept round to the head of the *spruit* on both sides of which the *donga* was formed, the South African Mounted Riflemen and more South African Police closed in, the Defence Force unit getting in rear and in flank of the rebels to cut them off. The attacking party had to work their way through open veld before they could charge the enemy; they made a mark as good as standing game. It was two and a half hours before the "Cease-fire" whistle sounded.

It fell to me to be a horse-holder (one man in each section is, of course, a horse-holder when mounted infantry are in action) in this fight. In nightmare I have passed that evening since—and wakened quickly, too. The worst of rifle fire is that you can hear bullets whizzing and spitting in trees, but it takes an experienced hand to divine direction. It was only afterwards I found out that a party of rebels were firing on our horses in rear. The horses knew it, though, and shewed it in their eyes. The sun came watery through the clouds just before sunset; I remember during the lulls in the wicked coughs of rifle fire hearing doves cooing gently in the sun-pierced trees.

When darkness fell we had captured Fourie, his brother and all his following, except nine men who made their escape at the beginning of the fight. The loyalist casualties in this action were twelve killed and twenty-four wounded. I saw a man who had shared a last cigarette with me as we rode into the action that afternoon lying dead on a blanket three hours later. In that instant I learnt something of the true meaning of war.

There are hundreds of brave deeds that must go unrecognised in these days. But from what I know of this particular action there was an amount of gallantry and quiet heroism displayed amongst the fellows

General Botha's train leaves the Orange Free State after the crushing of the Rebellion

Exhausted Troops after defeating De Wet in the Orange Free State

that deserved more than casual comment. I could speak of things I saw, and would like to, moreover. But as for my pains a punched head from outraged modesty would be the reward I shall say no more.

A few days later Fourie was tried by court-martial, convicted, and shot at dawn. In the last days of December the few remaining rebels at large either surrendered or were captured. As the last days of the Old Year slipped by, rebellion within the Union of South Africa died out, and General Botha spent the holidays in peace on his farm at Rusthof—in the haven where he fain would be.

LEAVING PRETORIA. GENERAL BOTHA'S BODYGUARD DEPARTING

KITS ABOARD. THE TROOPS DEPARTING FOR THE FRONT

CAMP OF THE BODYGUARD AT GROOTE SCHUUR

SECTION 1

The Preliminary Canter

At the stroke of seven on the evening of January 13, 1915, a train steamed out of Pretoria station to the accompaniment of roars of cheering. And few in the imposing string of carriages that made the train were sober within the meaning of the act. But everyone was in the highest spirits. The rebellion was over. The New Year was with us. After weary days our real business was on hand. We were off to German West at last.

We reached Cape Town on the 15th. I am particular about the date, not entirely as a result of a desire for meticulous accuracy. All who started on the South-West Campaign will remember their Cape Peninsula experience after the heat and burden of the rebellion. The authorities might have chosen most of our camping grounds about Cape Town with the genial purpose of providing a kind of military holiday as a preliminary canter to the campaign proper. The unit to which I was attached had its temporary resting place on the slopes of Table Mountain at Groote Schuur, on the Rhodes Estate. And I fancy the world has on its vast surface few spots more alluring and more bracing to the spirit.

Up till that time South Africa itself had never put an expeditionary army, to be shipped by sea, on a war footing, and at Cape Town the work of equipping the South-West African Expeditionary Force was carried on and finished during the four weeks we were there. The quiet pine and fir lined roads on the Rondebosch side of Table Mountain complained daily under the traffic of wagons and motors, horses, mules and guns; it ruined the roads and begot unceasing clouds of dust.

And from breakfast-time till late afternoon every street leading to

Cape Town and to the great Supply and Ordnance Stores at Maitland and at Portswood Road was filled with grey and khaki carts and wagons roaring steadily along in golden dust. In the whole Peninsula the normal interests of life were for the time being completely sidetracked.

Being associated directly with the Commander-in-Chief and Headquarters, we were fortunate in having our camp on the finest piece of ground on the estate; our tents stretched down a strip of sloping sward, sheltered from the wind by the wonderful trees that luxuriate on the lower falls of Table Mountain; from one's tent entrance the eye was caught by a panorama sweeping a radius of twenty miles inland. I shall never forget those days when in the morning wind and sun I helped to make out requisitions for shirts and breeches and saddlery to the notes of wood music; nor those nights when we lay in our blankets on the grass, stars swinging above, the town-lights winking away below us. It is not often in life that one slips into dreamless slumber on soft grass, lullabied by the night-song of a south-wester in pine trees centuries old.

If we had our discipline and our work at Cape Town, we had our compensations, too. At that time khaki was completely the fashion there. On the long promenade down Adderley Street to the pier-head you could have counted a dozen men in khaki to one in mufti. It reminded one of the days of the South African War fifteen years ago. There was naturally a tendency to make much of the soldier-visitor. It did not spoil him, though. A more orderly lot could not have been found. And this with the people whose guests we were in indulgent mood, and the civic authorities throwing open to us every amusement at their disposal.

Though there was work ahead we were all sorry to leave Cape Town.

On Friday, the 5th of February, we struck camp at sunrise. All our horses had been shipped the day before; we proceeded to the Docks by train and on foot. As showing the kindness with which the troops were treated I must mention that after the heavy work of embarking horses a body of one of the Ladies' War Organisations arranged refreshments for us at the railway station.

The journey by train from Groote Schuur to the City takes about fifteen minutes; by motor about a quarter of that time. But war-work is a trifle different; we were three hours on the heavily laden transport wagons before we got to the transport *Galway Castle*.

BROTHERS IN ARMS. THE BRITISH NAVY AND BOTHA'S BODYGUARD
FRATERNISED ABOARD. MANY OF THE LATTER ARE, OF COURSE, PURE
SOUTH AFRICAN

BOXING ABOARD. *EN ROUTE* TO GERMAN SOUTH-WEST AFRICA

Awaiting landing from the transport

Trekking over the terrible sand dunes near the coast, German South-West Africa

SOME OF THE FIRST *BURGHERS* TO LAND AT WALVIS

Many of us who have moved about a good deal and are fond of the sea were looking forward to that voyage. It was a four days' trip to Walvis Bay; we thought we would have rather a jolly time. Disillusion is hateful. And that trip was disillusionment itself. I suppose we inexperienced ones overlooked automatically the fact that we were in the ranks and travelling to war by transport. It wasn't a high-browed, superior outlook that caused our undoing, I fancy. The thing is, you must rough it soldiering by ship before you grasp the idea. There were other points, too.

When we got safely aboard the *Galway Castle* many of us fancied, in expressive phrase, that we were "well away"; that we had struck a good thing. Our officers were accommodated in befitting state in the first class; our warrants and staff non-commissioned dignitaries were also fixed up in correct style; the rest of us had plenty of room and quietness to ourselves in the third class. All this by 2.30 in the afternoon.

And then eighteen hundred more warriors filed down the quays and, like Mr. Jim Hawkins, came aboard, sir. Now most of these were as good fellows as you could wish for; but they were landsmen, such as never go down to the sea in ships. A large proportion, indeed, had never seen the sea before viewing it at Cape Town. (South Africa is a fair-sized territory.) Very few of them were good sailors. It is not a man's fault that he is not a good sailor; nor is he to blame for knowing little of the ways that make for cleanliness and comfort under even the most trying conditions on shipboard. But on the whole we did not enjoy that four days' voyage to Walvis Bay. It was a case of bedlam as to noise, and "muck in" and take what you can get.

Though my knowledge of organisation for a campaign is not great, I would suggest that for campaign work the only kind of ship used should be a vessel absolutely and completely fitted up as a troopship. If the ships the government used for the South-West campaign transport had all been fitted up uncompromisingly as "troopers" I fancy we should have fared better.

At 8 a.m. on the 9th we arrived at Walvis Bay. General Botha, who, with his chief of staff, A.D.C.'s, etc., had embarked at the Cape on the auxiliary cruiser *Armadale Castle*, arrived at Walvis later in the morning. We spent the day on board the *Galway Castle* awaiting orders and the disembarkation of horses.

Since the beginning of the operations in South-West Africa the world has been flooded with descriptions of Walvis Bay; at least I have seen two books with long descriptions of the place, and more than a dozen articles on the subject. I shall not add to this list by any long (and assuredly unconvincing) attempt at a new picture. When you have left the green-covered *kopjes* of the Cape a few days before and come to anchor in Walvis Bay on a cold morning you think you have reached No-man's-land after a fast voyage. It is a first impression only. The place is desolate enough; it suggests the Sahara run straight into the sea, or the discomforting dreariness of Punta Arenas, in Patagonia.

But first impressions are not everything. Walvis Bay is desolate; a study in yellow ochre sands, burnt sienna duns, tin shanties veiled in hot desert winds, and a sea that seldom knows anything more than a ripple. But that is the point. Walvis Bay is nothing now—but it is a bay. As a fact, it looks to be one of the finest natural harbours in the world. With the South-West interior developing in the future, Walvis Bay should have something to look forward to.

We left the *Galway Castle* on the 11th, disembarking into lighters, to be towed up the coast to the occupied German port of Swakopmund. Down to the tender, on to the lighter, kits and equipment, and farewell to the quietened steamer. For a while we stood away from her, and rose and fell under no way on the still grey waters. Then we saw a tender from the *Armadale Castle* steaming towards us. She came up on our starboard quarter and made fast. A figure well known to us all crossed the gangway and climbed to the boat-deck of our steam tender. We had not seen the commander-in-chief in personal command since the past bitter days of the rebellion. A great cheer hit the morning silence and echoed over the bay to each transport at anchor. With a smile of genuine pleasure, General Botha brought his hand to the salute. And away we went, the tender steaming full speed ahead, blunt-nosed barges surging in her wake, for Swakopmund.

Swakopmund was the first Headquarters of the Northern Force, Union Expeditionary Army; we made two sojourns at this German port. First we were there for a period of some five weeks, from February 11 till March 18, whilst awaiting the first advance into the Namib Desert; then we were there for a further month, from the 27th of March till the 25th of April, whilst awaiting the general advance to Windhuk and Karibib.

It is difficult to write about Swakopmund. As a town it is the most extraordinary place I have seen. I use the superlative deliberately. But I do not wish to live there. It is purely artificial, and artificial to a ghastly

BEFORE THE ADVANCE. GENERAL BOTHA PHOTOGRAPHED WITH THE
RED CROSS SISTERS

GENERAL BOTHA AND STAFF ALIGHTING FOR AN INSPECTION.
(THE FAMOUS BRIGADIER-GENERAL BRITS, WHO TREKKED TO
NAMUTONI, IS THE FOURTH FIGURE FROM THE RIGHT.)

degree too. There is not a spot of vegetation. There is not a genuine tree to be seen. The water has a detestable, unsatisfying blurred taste, to which the adjective "brackish" is applied. It is probable that a town occupied by enemy troops does not look at its best; but the fact that it was under such conditions when I first knew Swakopmund makes no important difference. The place in its essentials must always be the same. If ever there was a work of bluff Swakopmund is that thing. One fancies the German commercial expert, a government official, or, maybe, a representative of the ubiquitous Woermann, Brock & Co., looking along this ferocious and awful coast for a spot to found a town that should appear on the maps and be esteemed a seaport. The Swakop River? Very well. Was there water there? But certainly so; water obviously of the worst quality—yet water. Besides, were there not always refrigerators and condensing machinery? Upon which Swakopmund was forced into existence—planked down there bit by bit in the face of circumstance. Walk a trifle over a thousand yards from the edge of the changeful Atlantic through Swakopmund's deep sandy streets and you get the key to the town. For it ceases utterly, abruptly; from the door of its last villa, fitted with perfect furnishings from Hamburg, the bitter desolation that is the Namib Desert stretches away from your, very feet. Marvelling at this place, I was particularly struck by the size of its cemetery. But I was not long puzzled. If you strike Swakopmund on a fine sunshiny day you will be pretty favourably impressed with the climate; it seems warm and temperate, and the sun sparkles on the sea.

In a week or so you will learn to modify that judgment. More than half the days we were at Swakopmund a heavy pall of dampness hung over the place, and after a day or two of it one's system seemed to be badly affected. Maybe we were not acclimatised, but the fact remains that a very large proportion of us were down with a kind of dysentery, attended by vomiting and violent pains in the stomach. Then there are days when the winds blow from the desert—an indescribable experience. They bring moths and flies with them, and great clouds of sand; it is a genuine labour to breathe, and at noon and for two hours after the temperature in the sun runs up into the "hundred-and-sixties." Swakopmund is not a health resort; or perhaps we dwelt there in the wrong season, But it is a monument to Teutonic determination. The Germans willed this town there, planted it on the edge of the wilderness; fitted it out, from bioscope theatre to church with organ and electric organola; and they lived in it, with the climate of perdition

AWAITING THE ADVANCE.
THE COMMANDER-IN-CHIEF AT TEA WITH THE RED CROSS SISTERS

AWAITING THE ADVANCE. GARRISON SPORTS AT SWAKOPMUND.
START FOR 100 YARDS RACE

AWAITING THE ADVANCE. GARRISON SPORTS. WINNER

and all the accessories of a suburb of Berlin, and called it a seaport. It is not a seaport; in a fair gale you can't land a barrel of corks at the pier. But given time and they would have built in the face of nature a two million pounds breakwater and everything complete. Yes, they are a thorough people; they are human ants as regards work. Nevertheless, it is not colonising. The Germans are not colonists.

Army Headquarters were fixed at the Damaraland Building close to the shore—a splendidly equipped edifice, with a tower commanding a fifteen-mile-radius view of the desert and the sea. General Botha made the private quarters of the general officer commanding-in-chief at the Woermann Line House close by.

When we arrived at the northern seaport it had been in our possession many weeks, but our troops were occupying the trenches just outside the town, and from the Damaralands Building Tower our look-out and signallers could see through the heat-haze the enemy's patrols moving to and fro in the glistening sands beyond.

Whilst awaiting orders for an advance, life at Swakopmund was in some ways quite good. There were two attractions: regimental concerts, when sanctioned, and the shore. South Africa at war differs in great degree from other parts of the world. The country has the germ in its blood. Men who have campaigned before felt the stirring in them when the South-West campaign started. The call for volunteers acted like a magnet. All sorts and conditions of men were found with the Forces in the South-West. Patriotism called them; but there called them also that deep-seated spirit of unrest which prompts so powerfully when war drums sound once again. I used to think Kipling exaggerated a trifle; now I know the truth. At the concerts on the South-West front the most astonishing array of talent was to be found.

One such function in particular stands out in mind. The stage was made up of army biscuit boxes supporting rough planking outside a builder's yard in the deep sand. At a borrowed piano belonging to some vanished resident a trooper officiated; he was clothed in a grey back shirt and ammunition boots—and displayed the daedal methods of a Fragson. Singers of every type with every kind of voice, and perfectly trained, performed. Only later did I learn that amongst the artists were half a dozen of the best performers in Johannesburg. And at the foreshore, between fatigues, drills, and spells of duty the fellows used to gather, to enjoy the one luxury of Swakopmund—the surf-bathing. Here you would meet men upon whom you never expected again to set eyes assembled literally from all over South Africa from the

Swakopmund from the Lighthouse: Extreme Right

Swakopmund: Centre

Swakopmund: Extreme Left

Cape to the Zambesi. Belonging to one regiment I met, in privates and corporals, six well-to-do farmers, a handful of solicitors, bank clerks, a sub-native commissioner or two, and the no longer youthful private secretary to one of the most eminent semi-public companies in Africa. And there we all were cut off from the outside world. Each evening we got an issue of the official Bulletin— six square inches of paper thankfully received. For the rest we had no change from the perpetual sound of the sea and the mournful note of the bell-buoy that marks the inshore shoal. Its "*dong-dong, dong-dong-dong*" created a perfect illusion of the call to a tiny church through the country lanes of England. Everyone who was there can still hear the old bell-buoy at Swakopmund.

MAN AND BEAST IN THE DESERT: BOTH ABSOLUTELY SPENT

LOOKING FOR WATER IN THE RIVER BED

A HALT IN A RIVER BED: GENERAL BOTHA HAS LUNCH

The First Trek Into the Namib Desert

There were some skirmishes outside Swakopmund early in February. On the 23rd the commander-in-chief took the field; leaving the base shortly after dawn, he carried out a driving movement which pushed the enemy back from the outspan at Nonidas to his posts much further into the desert. In the course of this successful operation we first heard rumours that the Germans as a whole were not anxious to fight. The Union patrols captured several prisoners, amongst whom was an officer with whom I had several chats when I got the opportunity. As was the case with many of the prisoners afterwards taken, for a while he feigned total ignorance of English. It was not long before it became perfectly clear that he of course understood it well.

Following the operations on the 23rd of February, the mounted troops pushed steadily into the desert, occupying with merely nominal resistance Goanikontes, the water-hole and police post at Haigamkhab, and the water-hole at Husab.

On the 18th of March the commander-in-chief and staff, with all forces except those detailed to the base and infantry already holding the line and stores depots, etc., trekked out from Swakopmund on what was officially described as a "reconnaissance." It was really the first big push into the Namib Desert. The enemy had taken up an extremely strong position on the edge of the desert proper, on the front indicated on the general diagram of the campaign marked Pforte-Jakalswater-Riet.

I have little official knowledge on the tactics of the campaign; it is necessary, however, here to allude to the plan of proceeding known to every one who took any part in it. The vital consideration to the advance of any army across the Namib Desert is to secure the water-holes on the Swakop River. The Swakop is by no means the usual pre-possessing kind of stream that flows efficiently between wide banks. It flowed actually for a day just after General Botha landed at Swakop-mund— the first and last time, apparently, within the memory of man. But it has water in it nevertheless; and at fixed and charted spots are to be found bore-holes and wells for the convenience of dwellers in the profitless wilderness.

The principal wells and holes are at the places marked on the dia-gram. General Botha's principal task was to take an army right across the Namib Desert, and to do that he had to capture every water-hole and keep it. It is true that at certain points in the Swakop and other of the large rivers of South-West Africa you can find water by dig-ging very near the surface—perhaps. But when you have a parched army at your back you must deal as little as possible in speculation. At Riet and Jakalswater the enemy had determined to hold the valuable water-holes at any cost, but especially at Riet.

When General Botha treks he treks at express speed. With him the intention is that the essence of strategy shall be surprise. The com-mander-in-chief left Swakopmund at 2.30 a.m. on the 18th of March. We outspanned at Goanikontes, thirty-four kilos, at 10.30 that night. Goanikontes was left at 6.30 a.m., and the Husab Outspan was made at 10.20 that morning. The rest of the day was spent at Husab; at 6.30 in the evening the commander-in-chief, and with him General Brits, left for Riet, outspanned for a few hours and attacked the German position at Riet at dawn on the 20th. The general action which was fought on the Pforte-Jakalswater-Riet front on this day was conceiv-ably the most important move of the campaign. It was essential that the water-holes should be secured.

Around Riet, the principal point of attack and defence, the dispo-sition of the Germans was as strong as it is possible to imagine. My sketch of the place should give a fair idea of things. In the technical sense it is not a true plan; but accuracy is not sacrificed to clearness. The *veld* around the Riet water-holes is just a mass of small *kopjes* and rocks; it narrows to a small defile that opens suddenly on to the cov-erless Husab Road. This defile is the only main approach to the Riet wells, and it is commanded close up on both flanks—on the right by the great bare *kopje*, Langer Heinreich, on the other by small *kopjes* and a line of ridges.

In attacking this position General Botha had to consider not only

Main Guard aboard—*en route* to hunt the Huns

On the Great Trek—the Chief of the Staff has a hair-cut

ACTION AT RIET

the enemy's strength of position, but also the fact that his troops had to go into action after a waterless twenty-odd mile trek over the desert. As the commander-in-chief got up to his front on the 20th the big guns had started. The artillery duel continued well into the afternoon. Every credit is due to the other units, but it was our artillery that cracked the nut at Riet. The range was 2,700 yards; but the Germans never got it. Why it is difficult to say; they had every advantage, and one understands that the Germans are nothing if not artillerists. But they were a wash-out at Riet; they were over-firing the whole time. On the other hand, the Union gunners got the range at once and were all over the enemy. They put an ammunition wagon out of action after three shots, and did further deadly work. That afternoon General Botha sent a detachment out to attempt an enveloping movement. But they came back later, reporting that the slopes of Langer Heinreich on the right and the sharp *kopjes* on the left made the thing impossible.

As the afternoon came on I may say I don't think we knew too much about the state of affairs with the enemy, and when he ceased artillery fire about 3.30 p.m. everyone seemed pleased enough. Few knew then that the German commander had begun to evacuate the position; his supply of shells was said to have run short. On account of our numbers, also, he feared an enfilading movement on his left flank should our mounted infantry advance to the defile Q.

In the meantime the authorities had decided we must find water in the rear; for that purpose a party was at once despatched to Gawieb, in the Swakop River bed. It was found by a party from the commander-in-chief's bodyguard, and at the Gawieb Hole the greater part of the forces watered that night. And they took seven hours to do it.

Before sundown General Botha, with staff and bodyguard, fell back two miles on the Husab-Riet Road and camped there for the night. Scarcely had the Headquarters party arrived before news came that the enemy was in precipitate flight, had evacuated Riet and had blown up his small ammunition and railway water-tanks at the Riet terminus of the narrow gauge railway line to Jakalswater. Bodies of the Union troops had occupied Riet on the evening of the 20th.

The actions at the Jakalswater and Pforte fronts, to fight which the columns had swept away to our left the night before, were equally successful.

That is the general story of the fight of the 20th March on the inland edge of the Namib Desert. But how to picture vividly the scene before Riet that day? At dawn in those parts conditions are bearable enough; the sun has little strength; the night wind refreshes. From 6.30 till 10 o'clock the desert is endurable. Then comes the change. All along the front the stark yellow sand is taking on a different hue under the climbing sun rays. It turns almost to glaring whiteness all around— to where it stops short at the foot of those scorched and smothered rocks on the left flank. To our right the members of the Headquarters Staff are standing—sitting—resting. An officer brings his glasses down slowly, blinks, feels for a pipe, lights it. Another moves head and extended arm to the right and makes a remark to a colleague. Along the ridge we occupy the Bodyguard are standing-to and watching the action; you see that fellow wearily ease a heavy bandolier; further down another brings an army biscuit from his haversack and breaks it on his boot.

And now look at that little group almost straight ahead of us; as the tall chief-of-staff moves aside you see a figure on a little camp stool. The left hand is just under the hip, binoculars are in the right; up go both hands with the glasses; down they come. He speaks to the chief-of-staff; there is the favourite gesture—the arm is jerked out horizontally, the hand pointing loosely, and dropped again. The face is powdered with fine sand and dust; during the day he has been allowed a small beaker of water from the artillery. A favour indeed. That is Botha—Louis Botha, commander-in-chief, the man who leads us. And on either flank, well screened, little knots of men are grouped round the guns—and "*Hampang-ky-yao!*" they go in our ears, their report carrying ten miles back into the desert where our transport hears them in muffled thunder. And look up as you hear that screeching whistle. The enemy's shells burst in the depression behind us on both flanks— "*Pa-ha-ha.*" They look like slabs of cotton wool against the brazen blue sky. And all afternoon the heat strikes up at you overpowering, like the breath of a wild animal. Then the wind rises, and the sand shifts in eddies. Veils and goggles are useless. They can't keep out that spinning curtain of grit. The horses rattle the hard, dry bits in their mouths, trying to get some moisture.

On the 21st Headquarters moved into Riet. Here we found two water-holes in the bed of the river; one was a splendid Persian well, with chain buckets. Riet was no paradise; it was a luxury though, even if the river sand was blinding, to lie under a wagon and hear the water running.

Our casualties in the actions on the Pforte-Jakalswater-Riet front

AN UNIQUE PICTURE OF GENERAL BOTHA, THE COMMANDER-IN-CHIEF
AND HIS STAFF RECONNOITRING

AFTER RIET WATER IN BLESSED PROFUSION

were fifteen killed, thirty- nine wounded and forty-two missing. On the 21st our commandos occupied Salem, eight miles further up the Swakop River.

The commander-in-chief and his party remained at Riet till the 24th. It was then decided that a supply depot must be established at Riet before further advance was made. On the evening of the 24th Headquarters returned to Swakopmund, reaching the coast at 9.30 on the morning of the 26th—an extremely fast trek.

Looking out of my window in the heart of civilisation at the evening sun that glorifies the Pretoria green *kopjes*, the scene dissolves. In its place comes the picture of the first gaunt daylight on the 26th of March last at fifteen kilometres, just going into Swakopmund. The mist from the coast had rolled inland; through it after dawn came miles of horsemen and wagons, guns, limbers, lorries, ambulances. Every human unit in that column was covered in white dust, and every horse was weary. And except for the *staccato* "*click-click*" of bits and an occasional deep hum from a passing motor the army moved in perfect silence through the sand.

The official history of the South-West campaign remains to be written, of course; in the meantime I am convinced that the actions on the twenty-one mile Pforte-Jakalswater-Riet front were practically the deciding factors of the campaign.

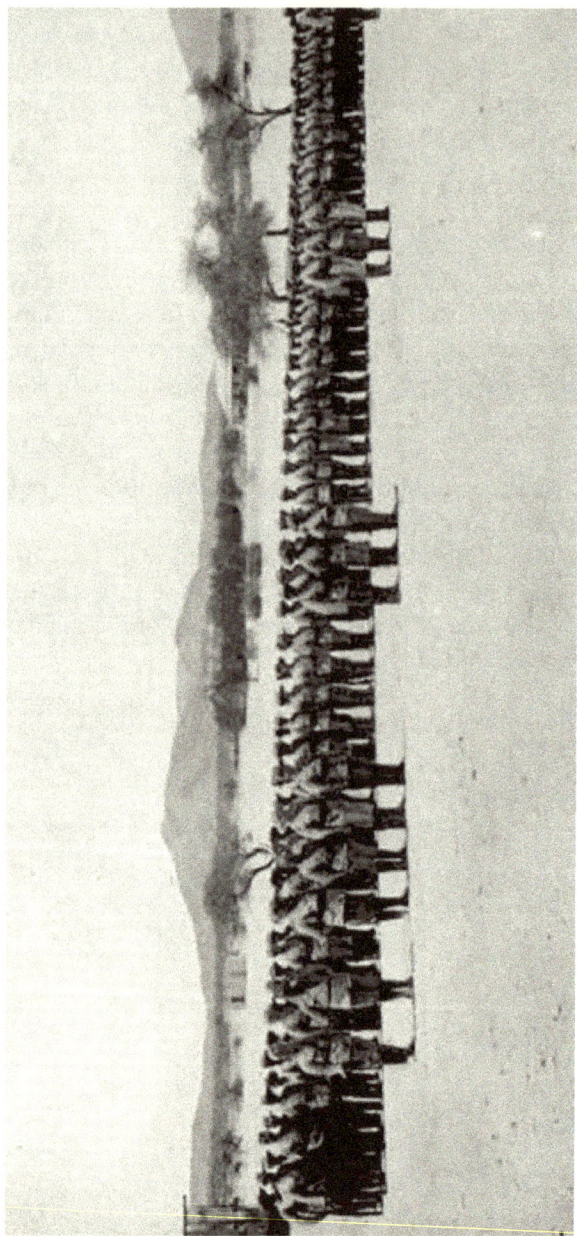

A Typical Parade of the Germans in South-West Africa

The Record Trek to Windhuk

On the 27th of March General Botha left Northern Force Head-quarters at Swakopmund for Luderitzbucht, the landing-place of the Central Force under the commands of Brigadier-General Macken-zie.

The whole plan of campaign was very much this. The Protector-ate was to be invaded from several angles, the route of these vari-ous forces being quite clear, I hope, in the diagram given. Roughly speaking there were three forces: the Northern (General Botha, Com-mander-in-Chief), working inland from Swakopmund; the Central (Brigadier-General Mackenzie) working inland from Luderitzbucht; and the Southern and South-Eastern converging on Keetmanshoop from Raman's Drift-Warmbad-Kalkfontein (Hartigan's Horse), from Upington (Brigadier-General van Deventer and Colonel Celliers) and from Kimberley-Hasuur (Colonel Berrange's column). As a re-sult of this great concentration on Keetmanshoop and northwards from all sides, the Germans would be forced to decisive action, to retreat northwards, or be cut off. Upon these forces reaching a certain distance inland a general move would be made in the direction of Windhuk—and again the enemy would have to fight or retreat to the limits of his railway system.

On the 30th of March the commander-in-chief returned to Swa-kopmund, and the same day news came of the occupation of Aus by the Central Force. It was now that we heard definitely that General Smuts was in the field with the forces south of us.

With the Central and Southern advances, General Mackenzie, from Luderitzbucht, occupied Garub on the 22nd of February, and Aus on March 31. Colonel Berrange's column, having left Hasuur on the 3rd of March, reached Kabus, by Keetmanshoop, on the 19th. Leaving

TYPICAL CAPTURED GERMAN INFANTRY

THE GREAT TREK. OTJIMBINGWE: ITS PALMS AND WELLS

Raman's Drift on the 2nd of April, Colonel Hartigan's column occupied Kalkfontein on the 14th of April, and reached Keetmanshoop on the 20th of April. Seeheim was occupied on the 18th of April. The advance to these towns was achieved by a series of fast treks in which frightful conditions of thirst and fatigue were encountered. General Mackenzie's troops in their advance north occupied Bethany on the 13th of April, and continued northward to Berseba, Gibeon, etc., on the way to Windhuk.

We now come to the feat that broke all known marching records and caused two hemispheres to talk. On Sunday and Monday, the 25th and 26th of April, General Botha's forces left the coast: on the 5th of May they were outside Windhuk. Striking right across the desert through every kind of country, General Botha's army marched night and day, and in five of those days covered a minimum distance of a hundred and ninety miles. Many units did much more than two hundred miles—over forty miles per day.

It was some trekking.

Swakopmund was left on the 26th of April at dawn. Haigkamchab was reached by I on the same afternoon, and Husab supply base at 6.30 p.m. Next day Husab was left at 2.15 p.m.; the column halted for a few minutes at 5 p.m., and pushed right through to Riet, which was made at 10.20 that evening. Headquarters rested all day on the 28th at Riet, left it at 8 p.m., trekked by moonlight along the Swakop River for three hours, outspanned till an hour before dawn, and made Salem at 6.45 a.m. on March 29. At 9.30 that morning the column moved on again, reached outspan at twenty miles by 1.35 in the afternoon, rested for an hour and a half and pushed on again till a quarter before midnight, when it rode into Wilhelmsfeste. But the water was at Kaltenhausen, some miles further ahead of this military post. We reached it at 1.15 on the morning of the 30th. Animals took two hours to water in the bitterly cold morning air. The guards had not taken two steps on their beat before the sand was littered with sleepers that looked like dead men. These sleeping columns, some ninety to a hundred miles from the coast, were now halfway to Windhuk.

Two hours after daylight General Headquarters moved to a camping ground two miles back towards Wilhelmsfeste (Tsaobis), and rested during the day in the shade of the scant trees with which the *veld* was covered as the desert was left behind. The rest of the Northern Army had trekked on with scarcely any pause. Shortly before sunset, the commander-in chief set out on a night march of twenty odd miles

THE GREAT TREK. OTJIMBINGWE: THE COMMANDER-IN-CHIEF AT THE OLD GERMAN CAPITAL

THE GREAT TREK. GETTING MILK FROM A GOAT. MILK WAS PRICED BEYOND SILVER

to Otjimbingwe. The trek was done at a fierce pace till midnight, when an outspan was ordered; the party slept for four hours, and made Otjimbingwe just as the dawn of the 1st of May was breaking. As General Botha rode into this old mission settlement the rear of the German forces, closely pursued, was galloping in retreat over the *kopjes* to the east. Many prisoners were taken here.

General Botha spent the day at Otjimbingwe, left at dawn on the 2nd, and trekked north-west seventeen miles to Pot Mine, which he reached at 12.45 p.m. Here the commander-in-chief awaited the arrival of General Smuts, had a conference with him, and moved in force on Karibib at 2 a.m. on the 5th of May. He trekked the whole of that day, with two halts of an hour each, and entered Karibib on the heels of the enemy at five o'clock in the afternoon. At the same time the rest of the Northern Force had entered Okasise, Okahandja, Waldau, and other stations on the railway, had captured the whole system practically up to Omaruru, and were at the gates of Windhuk. The German forces were in full retreat to the north and north-east. Their civilian populations, left behind in the towns, seemed dumfoundered at the appearance of the Union troops. Meantime the Southern and Central Armies had approached the German capital on the southern flank.

This account of the advance through the desert of General Botha's Northern Force is purposely bald. The process of a vast flooding of water over a country is in essence bald and direct. And that is as near as I can get for comparison. General Botha's advance was like a well-ordered flood: which, I take it, was exactly the idea. At a fixed time organised bodies of men, mounted, dismounted and with artillery, were systematically poured over the German territory. I am sure most of the fellows who took part in that advance and recall it in detail will in the future look back and wonder. For it is a subject for wonder, even if history does contain some marches more eventful. It has been stated since that all transport was left behind. But that is not strictly true: a large quantity of transport was brought on by the Union Forces; passed through the deepest sand in waterless desert, between gorges, over big *kopjes*, into almost trackless *bushveld*—and was never more than a day and a half behind. At one place out of a convoy of twenty-seven wagons, seventeen capsized.

It is hackneyed, I know, but there is only one way to describe the great trek to Windhuk. It was absolutely "a chequer-board of nights and days." Looking at my diary just now, that I have had ten years'

THE GREAT TREK. AN EXTEMPORE BATH TOWARDS THE
END OF THE TREK

practice at keeping, I see a confusion got into the dates. You didn't know anything about the date or the day of the week. Existence was just a dateless alternation of light and darkness, of saddle-up and off-saddle, of cossack-post, of thinking about water—and of yearning with every fibre of one's being for the ineffable boon of a long sleep.

It will be seen that the key to the advance over the Namib Desert was the Swakop River. The water-holes of the Swakop River are very singular; they form the nucleus of a kind of settlement (even if it be only a couple of small huts) right in the dry river bed. At Kalten-hausen, to take but one example, there is a splendid shooting-lodge slap bang in the centre of the river; it has a fine courtyard walled and railed in. It seemed extraordinary. At these water-holes you suddenly leave the stony sand of the desert and come on to finest soft sand. It is quite pleasant at night, but day tells another story. Just after sunrise a wind starts blowing down the river valley and raises this superfine, mineralised sand. To lie exposed to this for a day is an awful experi-ence; the fine dust will penetrate anywhere. I am sure it must lead to positive blindness in time.

I mentioned the water-holes of the Swakop River for the par-ticular reason that their situation in most cases adds immensely to the merit of the Northern Army's great trek. The trek-road from Swa-kopmund follows the river only in a broad sense; the Haigamkhab, Husab and Gawieb water-holes are really three to four and five miles from the road and the camping grounds. That is to say, the columns, after a twenty mile trek in the sand and sun had another quarter of the distance to go—*to water*. And to water usually means across the yard to the troughs, so to speak. We shall remember the water-holes of South-West Africa. There is many a fellow now back in civilisation who can recall vividly the tramp over stony, loose gravel through those great echoing rocks down to the water-holes at Haigamkhab, Husab and Gawieb.

Hour after hour the processions of weary riders passed each other in a cloud of dust that rose five hundred yards and filled the chok-ing canyon. The invariable question from him going wearily to water to him coming refreshed and smothered in water-bottles and with a livelier horse from it: "Is it far, boy?" And the stereotyped answer of encouragement was as always: "No, no; just round the corner." All these water-holes are almost duplicates of each other. I suppose not the echo of a bird now hurts their pristine and awful quietude.

The marvellous series of changes as one advances constitutes the

A Beauty Spot passed during the last Trek

The Last Phase. Conference at Omaruru. German Staff lunching

The general receives his bodyguard at a garden party after return

most striking feature of the advance to Windhuk from the coast. By rail it is not so striking; but taking the marching route *via* the Swakop River water-holes—Swakopmund, Nonidas, Haigamkhab, Husab, Riet, Salem, Wilhelmsfeste (Tsaobis), Otjimbingwe, Windhuk—the changes in the country and the stages that show them are as palpable as if marked by a system of parallel walls. I have never seen this feature of the *veld* so marked elsewhere in South Africa.

Swakopmund is the limit in the down-grade— deep sand; *brak* water; a treacherous, dreary climate, with visitations of furnace-heat desert winds; a huge cemetery; moths and flies. From Nonidas to Haigamkhab and Husab the sand lightens and hardens, the atmosphere improves, rocks, barren *kopjes* begin to appear; the little water you get is fairly good. Riet comes; the barren *kopjes* are more frequent; the atmosphere, hot in the day, is beautiful by night; the water is perfect. Salem is a duplicate Riet; a small settlement in the river bed; but the water is more plentiful, the vegetation more profuse. Then comes the great trek to Tsaobis.

It does not look far on the map; it is a huge stretch nevertheless. For the first three hours it was Riet-Salem country with extensions and additions. Vast gorges, black and brown *kopjes*, boulders, sand stretches, clumps of bush, minute trees. And then, on Thursday the 29th of April (memory holds the date like a vice), we saw grass. It was grass. It was undoubtedly grass—the kind of grass that gave one the feeling that this particular *veld*, like a man prematurely bald through worry or riotous living, had been trying some hair restorer with ludicrous results—grass whitish, feeble, attenuated, that to be seen at all wanted an eye levelled along the ground.

Each half hour brought its surprise as we moved along, General Botha on his white horse at the head of the column, just visible to the eye through the thick curtain of white dust our horses' feet flung up into the sun glare. We rode in great gorges between *kopjes*. We crossed dry river courses. We clattered over the hard bosoms of rocks, switchbacked up and down each hour working out of the desert. Trees began to appear—caricatures of trees. Then game spoor was reported. And suddenly, just after noon, rain fell—out of one cloud in a sky otherwise brazenly clear five drops fell. I counted five on my bridle hand.

Rain on the edge of the Namib Desert. It was ludicrous, too bizarre; it was the last straw. We gasped. A deep roar of ironical cheering went up. The commander-in-chief looked round and laughed. When we outspanned later the horses made a show of grazing for the first

GERMAN PRISONERS OF WAR, IMPRISONED AT KARIBIB

KARIBIB

TOWARDS WINDHUK. THE FIRST TROOPS IN WALDAU

The first South African Engineer Corps Staff at Windhuk

time for five months. The sagacious animals showed plain amazement in their eyes. At Wilhelmsfeste (Tsaobis) the *bushveld* begins. The water supply of Otjimbingwe is the feature of that rather quaint settlement. One must ever associate it with its fine aeromotor pumping the precious fluid for parched man and beast to drink their full after the desert passage in the shade of cool palms many years old.

During the great trek alarms regarding mines were most frequent. There were many wonderful escapes. It seems a marvel that the enemy were not more successful than they were with these deadly machines. Suffer casualties we did; but if all the mines that were laid had blown up our casualties would have been formidable indeed. But somehow those mines seemed foreordained not to act. They were discovered by the merest chance; or they failed to go off; or they exploded at the wrong time.

Making for Karibib in the forenoon of the 5th of May, the authorities naturally showed the greatest caution for the safety of General Botha— though a large body of Union mounted troops had passed over the same ground before the commander-in-chief, staff and body-guard traversed the road.

In view of the fact that the South African Army was operating against the forces of the same nation that has ravaged and despoiled Belgium, a point should be made here. It must be remembered that the armed forces of the Protectorate simply cleared bag and baggage out of all the important inland towns in the face of Botha's overwhelming advances. They left wife and child, the old and infirm, every stick of property they could not carry, at our mercy. When we entered Karibib at five in the evening the non-combatant population were moving about the streets, or standing in best bib and tucker at their doors, calmly gazing at the trek-stained horsemen that sought the nearest water tanks. They had not the slightest fear of us. I spoke to a comrade who has seen war aforetime. He said he had never seen a more orderly occupation of a town.

The conduct of the South African troops should assuredly be noted. The very confidence of these German townspeople that they had nothing to fear from the hated troops of the British Union of South Africa was eloquent. The thing stood out, a piece of bitterest irony in connection with a people whose kindred across the seas were making civilisation shudder at their atrocities afloat and ashore. The news of the *Lusitania* massacre on the high seas reached Karibib just after occupation. Did one Teuton in the place have to suffer as a consequence

Towards Windhuk. A quick railway repair after the Germans' usual practice of blowing up railway bridges

Towards Windhuk. The first train to Windhuk. The South African Engineer Corps Construction Party aboard

even the insult of a word? No. What would the Germans have done? General Botha's forces had crossed a desert through which it was the open boast of the enemy that it was strewn with mines and with every well poisoned. Was a single defenceless citizen of Windhuk or Karibib the worse for it after the occupation? Not one. The greater part of General Botha's forces were on a half—a quarter— an eighth rations when they made Karibib, Okahandja, Okasise, Waldau and the capital; they lived until all supplies could come up on less than one biscuit a day, a pinch or two of meal, and fresh meat.

How much looting occurred in these towns?

There was none worthy the name.

Everyone was guarded. A few hours after the places were entered the orders were issued threatening severe and instant penalties should any looting be done by the hungry troops; officers, etc., were quietly billeted; and to the houses occupied by women and marked with a white cross no one unauthorised was allowed any approach whatsoever.

It was magnanimous, it was magnificent. But I wonder if the chivalrous Teuton would call it war!

Karibib, the practical junction of the railway running north to Grootfontein, the enemy's new "capital," was made Army Headquarters. General Botha hoisted the flag at Karibib and proclaimed it on the 6th of May, spent a few days settling matters at Karibib, and on the afternoon of the 11th set out for Windhuk by motor, formally to enter the capital. With him the Commander-in-Chief took his Chief of Staff (Colonel Collyer), Lieut.-Colonel de Waal (Provost Marshal), Major Bok (Military Secretary), Major Trew (Officer Commanding Bodyguard), Major Liepoldt (Chief Intelligence Officer), Major Esselen (Staff), an escort from the 4th Battery South African Mounted Riflemen and Bodyguard. Overnight the Headquarters party "outspanned" at Okasise on a beautiful camping-ground, and, meeting the Burgomaster of Windhuk under some trees outside the town, ran into the South-West capital towards noon.

Later in the day the ceremony of formal taking over was performed before a big crowd at the *Rathaus*. It was in every way a historic scene. The mounted troops lined all about the square that fronts the *Rathaus* from the roadway, their weary horses and stained uniforms showing up in the background, with the throng of civilians crowded amongst the motor-cars and carts in the square itself. A warrant-officer of the commander-in-chief's bodyguard had the honour of hoisting the

AT WINDHUK. HOW WE TREAT THE GERMAN WOMEN. TEN MINUTES AFTER OCCUPATION

AT WINDHUK. THE COMMANDER-IN-CHIEF ADDRESSES HIS MASSED TROOPS FROM THE *RATHAUS*

Union Jack over the *Rathaus* at Windhuk, the capital of Germany's erstwhile colonial possessions.

A cheer went up as the flag fluttered up in the noon sunlight. Windhuk was naturally regarded as the Mecca, so to speak, of the invading army.

With the interests of the civilised world fixed on the vast slaughter-grounds of Europe, I shall not spend much time describing Windhuk. It is a pretty, picturesque little town, built amongst brown and purple hills. In most ways it is highly finished; reflects the spirit of German thoroughness that is an admitted attribute of the race. As usual in South-West Africa, it has nothing of the *colonial* town about it; it might be another suburb of Berlin. Many of the houses are thoroughly built into the sides of the surrounding *kopjes*—perched like great red-roofed cages on the hillsides. The place doesn't seem to have a single industry of its own; but then, as I said elsewhere, there is hardly an established industry in the Protectorate.

There is one thing about Windhuk that grips your attention—and holds it in no uncertain manner, too. One of the great objectives of the South-West campaign was to secure the Windhuk wireless station. When you see this—catch a glimpse of it suddenly where it stands on the *veld* outside the town—you get a thrill of sheer astonishment. The thing seems monstrous there. It is foreign to our ideas—a wireless colossus in such a place. Had I seen this vast piece of work in a humming city that stands warden to the seas it would have fitted in. But where it is—well, it just surprised. Fancy a pretty *bijou veld* town, red roofs, neat church, pepper trees, aeromotors, sleepy people and everything—and across the *veld*, a mile and a half away, darkening the sky with great vertical lines, five terrific steel lattice pillars, nearly four hundred feet high, tied by cables with stay bolts as big as a man; their aerials sweep from pillar to pillar, answer to the wind the deepest note of a giant 'cello, and eavesdrop and conjure amongst the news markets of the world. Now there is no electric light in this village of Windhuk, or Windy Corner, yet. What was the idea with this stupendous thing? And there are not enough Germans in the place—or in the whole territory, if it comes to that—to populate a good-sized town. There is also the usual telegraphic communication to the coast, etc. Yet—the wireless.

Its significance could be of one kind only: a military one.

Leaving the town in the hands of Colonel Mentz, Military Governor, and Lieut.-Colonel de Waal, the commander-in-chief returned to Headquarters at Karibib on the 14th of May.

AT THE GATE OF WINDHUK. HEADQUARTERS STAFF MOTORS
AWAITING ENTRY

AT THE GATE OF WINDHUK. GENERAL BOTHA DISCUSSES
MATTERS WITH THE GOVERNOR OF WINDHUK

AT THE GATE OF WINDHUK. THE INTERPRETER

AT THE GATE OF WINDHUK. GENERAL BOTHA EMPHASISES

THE GREAT WIRELESS STATION AT WINDHUK
(Note the size of the man as he rests on one of the
foundations of the vast derricks)

CONFERENCE AT OMARURU. GENERAL STAFF LUNCHING

THE LAST PHASE. THE BE2 TUNING UP IN SHED BEFORE FLIGHT OVER GERMAN POSITIONS

AT THE PROVOST MARSHAL'S OFFICE AT WINDHUK—ALL IN LAW AND ORDER

THE UNION JACK JUST HOISTED AT THE GOVERNOR'S OFFICE, WINDHUK

THE GREAT MILITARY BARRACKS AT WINDHUK

The Last Phase

On the 19th of June Brigadier-General Brits, of the Northern Army, occupied Omaruru, on the Karibib-Grootfontein line. The enemy had retreated.

Nearly five weeks had passed since the commander-in-chief had officially proclaimed the capital. During this time much had happened. An abortive conference had taken place at Omaruru itself, the Germans, we were informed afterwards, asking for terms that we were in no mind to give them. The railway line between Swakopmund and Karibib, broken up by dynamited bridges, had been to a great extent repaired. The poorly rationed troops were now replenished. The horses, badly knocked up after the rush through to Windhuk, had had opportunity to mend a bit. General Botha had proclaimed the country; with refreshed troops and horses, he was setting out to attempt to spring a final surprise on the Germans. He had now the Aviation Corps in full working order—had aerial eyes wherewith to be guided through a subtropical bush country very full of possible dangers. He had ahead of him an enemy astonished, yet, if what was rumoured was true, prepared to make a series of fights and a big stand in country of his own choice. He had with him an army that had crossed a desert and, arriving in bush country such as you find in the Rhodesia "low" *veld*, knew the nature of it as only the South African can.

On June 24 Headquarters ran into Kalkfeld just after midnight. The enemy had retreated. It had been predicted with the utmost confidence that the Germans would here put up a fight. So confidently was this expected that the commander-in-chief would hardly believe it when the aeroplanes returned and reported that there were about half a dozen Germans left in the place. Yet that proved to be exactly the fact, and so greatly impressed was General Botha with the accu-

Windhuk Panorama

Point of Entry of Gen. Botha   Railway Statⁿ.

Gov^t. Build^{gs}.   Church

Provost Marshall's Q^{rs}.   Rathaus

PANORAMA OF WINDHUK

racy of the observations on this occasion that he emphasised that the skymen were to receive every possible assistance for the future.

On June 26 Headquarters arrived at Okanjande, and pushed through to Otjiwarongo, arriving there at 12 noon. The pace of the trekking was now becoming phenomenal, and though the country was quite good, water was as scarce as ever, the bush being intensely dense, with thick sweet grass as much as eight feet high in places. It was a country made for ambushes. In less than a week General Botha had trekked over one hundred and twenty miles, the distance from Karibib to Otjiwarongo. During this trek the army had had water only twice on the stretch from Omaruru. But delay of any kind was now highly undesirable: the columns could not afford to pause long owing to the consumption of rations. It was no part of the Commander-in-Chief's policy to make bases and await the arrival of large supplies; water was uncertain, and congestion of columns at the watering places had to be avoided as much as possible.

Near Okanjande the first great development in General Botha's final strategy occurred. The northern advance was being conducted as follows. Brigadier-General Brits, on the left, remained at Otjitasu, leaving it on June 30. General Botha, with his command, in the centre, was holding to the narrow gauge Karibib-Otavi-Tsumeb-Grootfontein Railway, and General Myburgh's column to the right. Brigadier-General Brits now branched away to Otjitasu, making for Outjo, Okanknejo, and across the Etoscha Pan to Namutoni. The other columns moved on, trekking night and day, as in the great advance across the Namib Desert.

Headquarters made Okaputa on June 29; paused the next day, and on July 1 the Staff, leaving Okaputa at 8 o'clock in the morning, reached Otavi and Otaviafontein at 4.30 p.m., close on the heels of an engagement at Osib between the Germans and Brigadier-General Manie Botha, who had pushed on with the Orange Free State Brigade at 6.30 the previous evening, June 30. This engagement took place in the now intensely thick bush country. In defeating the enemy, at a cost of a dozen casualties, Brigadier-General Manie Botha succeeded in securing the finest water supply the Union Forces had yet seen, and so swift and resolute was the fighting of the *burghers* that the enemy fled to their last strong-hold northward towards Tsumeb. Before striking the enemy in this action the Free State Brigade, and their accompanying batteries from the 2nd South African Mounted Riflemen, had trekked forty-two miles in sixteen hours without halt for any kind

PICTURESQUE WINDHUK: PHOTOGRAPH SHOWING THE HOUSES NESTLING
IN THE HILLS, TAKEN FROM THE CHURCH.

WINDHUK. BASKING IN THE SUN: FROM THE GREAT WIRELESS STATION

HOW THE GERMANS STARTED TO TRY TRADING WITH US TEN MINUTES
AFTER WE ENTERED THE CAPITAL. NOTE THE SPELLING

of a rest. Behind them, in support, came the force, consisting of the 6th Mounted Brigade, with the 1st South African Mounted Riflemen Batteries, who did a similar trek, through thickest bush, covering almost fifty miles in twenty hours. And the animals had come through from Karibib—almost two and a half degrees of latitude south.

At the same time as Brigadier-General Manie Botha had left Okaputa, Brigadier-General Lukin, with the 6th Mounted S.A.M.R. Brigade, had left Omarasa. We had therefore a perfect network of highly mobile forces advancing on the German position somewhere north. Away on the right, from Windhuk and Okahandja through the Waterberg, was Brigadier-General Albert's column. On his left was Brigadier-General Myburgh. Nearer the railway was Brigadier-General Manie Botha. Next came the commander-in-chief with headquarters staff and bodyguard; and, further, General Lukin. For the time being Brigadier-General Brits, on the extreme left, had disappeared.

Brigadier-General Manie Botha now advanced right into the bush, supported by Brigadier-General Lukin, who occupied Eisenberg Nek, on the right flank. Brigadier-General Myburgh, trekking by forced marches, in the course of his flanking movement on the right cut the line between Otavi and Grootfontein, and, swerving north, encountered the enemy at Asis and Gaub. This column, having captured seventy Germans, marched straight on to Tsumeb, the extreme northerly limit of the railway, forty miles north of Otavi. Here the enemy was attacked so resolutely that they surrendered with all arms and four field guns, and the Union prisoners of war were released. And great was their rejoicing, too. Other columns marching north had now reached Rietfontein and Grootfontein.

It so arose now that General Myburgh, having got for a brief space out of touch with the Commander-in-Chief, was not aware that the Germans had opened, on July 5, negotiations with General Botha. General Myburgh was at once communicated with. As a fact, at the time he entered Tsumeb, a conference was on hand farther south.

Why did the German forces in the Protectorate surrender without making the big stand they threatened? If any proof be needed that they did intend to make a stand it is necessary only to glance at the plan of their final dispositions. And that is just where General Botha and his forces had done their work. There is not the least doubt, not the very least, that von Franke might have made a stand. It would have been nothing more than a quixotically honourable waste of life ending in one only possible way.

The Last Phase. Difficulties with General Botha's car through the thick sand

The Last Phase. The Germans had a hobby of blowing up bridges. Here is a fine specimen

GENERAL FRANK'S HOUSE, WINDHUK. PHOTO OF THE TWO FIRST MEN
THERE TAKEN UNDER THE FLAG HAULED DOWN BY US

WINDHUK. THE FIRST BRITISH STATION-MASTER AND ONE OF HIS STAFF

He was surrounded before he knew it.

So neat and swift had been the scheme prepared by the Com-mander-in- Chief that the German was incredulous—until his scouts kept coming in and telling him what the real state of affairs was. For Brits, after a two hundred mile detour through the wildest country had swept right north to Namutoni on the Great Etoscha Pan, had released more prisoners and was swerving further out. Myburgh was in Tsumeb. Both these generals were behind the Germans, ready to strike out forthwith; and von Franke was cut off from all his supplies. He had simply been caught—caught by remorseless forced marches and strategy as neat as a trivet—in a great fork with bent prongs. On the sketches in this little book, to which I have sacrificed everything possible for clearness, the general simple scheme of the campaign may be apparent. The final position on July 5 was something like the dia-gram over the page.

At kilometre 500 on the line between Otavi and Korab, at 2 a.m. on the 9th of July 1915, von Franke, the German Commander, and Dr. Seitz, the Imperial Governor of South-West Africa, discreetly sur-rendered to Louis Botha, Commander-in-Chief and Prime Minister of the Union of South Africa.

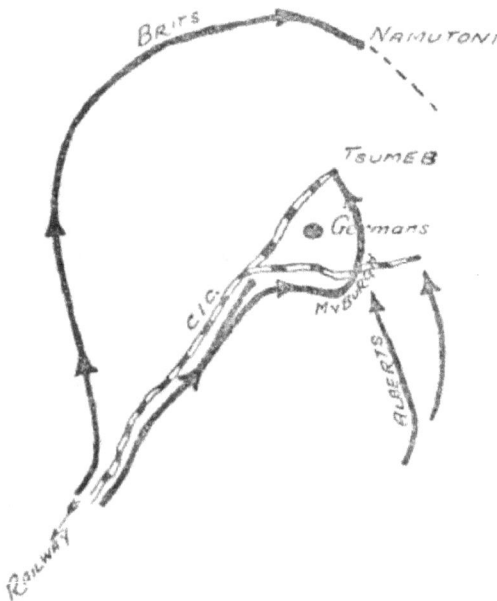

SOUTH-WEST AFRICA. POSITION OF ENEMY BEFORE SURRENDER

THE LAST PHASE. OPPOSITE THE VERY SPOT WHERE
SURRENDER WAS MADE. A VAST ANT-HILL AT 500 KILOMETRES

— South West F

— Position of Enemy Before

Usib

Enemy Camps

Scale. 1 58 Miles to 1 Inch

From Otjo to Otari

From Otjo Junction

Enemy Troops. • Enemy Schlff.
— Trenches. • Bn OS Pet

THE LAST PHASE. THE GERMAN WHITE FLAG TRAIN JUST ARRIVING

THE LAST PHASE. GENERAL BOTHA MEETS VON FRANKE AT 500 KILOMETRES

THE LAST PHASE. TROOPS ENTRAINING TO RETURN HOME

THE LAST PHASE. THE FAMOUS RHODESIAN REGIMENT THAT DID SO
MUCH IN THE FINAL BRILLIANT MOVEMENT

THE LAST PHASE. ISUMEH. BRITISH PRISONERS RELEASED

Appendix

Pretoria, July 10.

The terms of surrender of the military forces of the Protectorate of German South-West Africa, as agreed to by the Government of the Union of South Africa, and accepted by his Excellency Dr. Seitz, the Imperial Governor of the Protectorate of German South-West Africa, the commander of the military forces, which was signed on the 9th of July, 1915, are that—

(1) The military forces of the Protectorate of German South-West Africa (hereinafter referred to as the Protectorate) remaining in the field under arms and at the disposal and the command of the commander of the said Protectorate forces, are hereby surrendered to General the Right Hon. Louis Botha, Commander-in-Chief of the Forces of the Union of South Africa in the field. Brigadier-General H. T. Lukin, C.M.G., D.S.O., acting on behalf of General Botha, shall be the officer in charge with arranging details of the surrender and giving effect to it.

(2) The active troops of the said forces of the said Protectorate surrendered in terms of paragraph (1) shall, in the case of officers, retain their arms and may give parole, being allowed to live each under that parole at such places as he may select. If for any reason the Government of the Union is unable to meet the wish of any officer as regards choice of abode, the officer concerned will choose some place in respect of which no difficulty exists. In the case of other ranks of the active troops of the said forces of the Protectorate, such other ranks shall be interned under proper guard at such place in the Protectorate as the Union Government shall decide upon.

(3) Each non-commissioned officer and man of the ranks last referred to shall be allowed to retain their rifles, but no ammunition. One officer shall be permitted to be interned with the other ranks of artillery, and one with the other ranks of the remainder of the active troops, and one with the other ranks of the police.

(4) All reservists (*Landwehr*) of all ranks of the said forces of the Protectorate now remaining under arms in the field shall, except to the extent as is provided for in paragraph (6) below, give up their arms upon being surrendered, in such formations as may be found most convenient, and after signing the annexed form of parole shall be allowed to return to their homes and resume civil occupation.

(5) All reservists (*Landwehr* and *Landsturm*) of all ranks of the said forces of the Protectorate who are now held by the Union Government as prisoners of war taken from the forces of the Protectorate, upon signing the form of parole above mentioned in paragraph (4), shall be allowed to resume civil occupation in the Protectorate.

(6) Officers of the Reserve (*Landwehr* and *Landsturm*) of the said forces of the Protectorate who surrender in terms of paragraph (1) above shall be allowed to retain their arms, provided they sign the parole above mentioned in paragraph (4).

(7) All the officers of the said forces of the Protectorate who sign the form of parole above mentioned in paragraph (4) shall be allowed to retain their horses, which are nominally allotted to them in the military establishment.

(8) The Police of the Protectorate shall be treated, as far as have been mobilised, as active troops. Those members of the Police who are on duty on distant stations shall remain at their posts until relieved by the Union troops, in order that the lives and property of non-combatants may be protected.

(9) Civil officials in the employment of the German Government of the Protectorate shall be allowed to remain in their homes provided they sign the parole above mentioned in paragraph (4). Nothing, however, in this statement to be construed as entitling any such official to exercise the functions of the appointment which he holds in the service of either of the Governments aforesaid, or to claim from the Union Govern-

ment the emoluments of such appointment.

(10) With the exception of the arms retained by the officers of the Protectorate forces and by other ranks of the active troops, as provided in paragraph (2), all war material (including all field guns, mountain guns, small arms and guns, and small arm ammunition), and the whole of the property of the Government of the Protectorate, shall be placed at the disposal of the Union Government.

(11) His Excellency the Imperial Governor shall appoint a civil official of the Protectorate Service who shall hand over and keep a record of all Government property of the Civil Departments, including records which are handed over to the Union Government in terms of paragraph (10), and the Commander of the said forces of the Protectorate shall appoint military officers, who shall hand over and keep a similar record of all Government Property of the Military Department of the Protectorate.

Given under our hand this 19th day of July 1915.

(Signed)   Louis Botha,
General Commanding-in-Chief of the Union Forces in the Field.

Seitz,
Imperial Governor of German South-West Africa.

Franke,
Lieut.-Colonel, Commander of the Protectorate Forces of German South-West Africa.

The form of parole, shown as an annexure, begins—

I, the undersigned, hereby place myself on my honour not to re-engage in hostilities in the present war between Great Britain and Germany.

TOTAL UNION CASUALTIES.

The official report shows that the total casualties of the operations in South-West Africa in connection with the Union Forces are approximately as follows—

Killed in action	88
Died of wounds	25
Wounded in action	263
Wounded and taken prisoners	48

Unwounded prisoners in hands of enemy	612

Total	1,036
Died of disease	97
Died through accidents and by misadventure	56

Total	153

Total Enemy Surrenders

Immediately after the capitulation of the enemy, Brigadier-General Lukin reported that he had satisfactorily completed the work of accepting surrenders. The total number of surrenders amounted to 4,410, made up as follows—

Officers of the Active Troops and Police	110
Officers of the Reserve	177
Rank and File of Active Troops and Police	1,548
Rank and File of Reserve	2,575

The Union Forces when at greatest strength numbered 50,000 men.

The Germans when at full strength numbered 9,000, but a proportion of these consisted of civilians, who eventually refused to serve.

Amendment

In an official *communiqué* issued at the end of July, figures were given of the total number of the enemy included in the general surrender. The total then given was 4,410, and included the surrender of the main body at Korab, and also troops captured by Brigadier-General Myburgh at Tsumeb on July 6, the surrenders at Grootfontein, Otavifontein, Otavi and Tsumeb, and those who surrendered at Otjiwarongo.

The additional numbers captured or surrendered at various points since General Botha made his advance northwards after occupation of Windhuk are—

To Brigadier-General Myburgh's force, mostly at Gaub	105
To Brigadier-General Manie Botha's force between Okaputa and Otavifontein	50
To Brigadier-General Lukin's force	12
To Brigadier-General Brits' force, mostly at Namutoni	163

Total	330

Thus the total number of prisoners taken during the last stage of the campaign, *viz.* from June 18 to July 9, was 4,740.

THE GERMAN STAFF BEFORE SURRENDER

GENERAL BOTHA AND HIS BRILLIANT CHIEF OF STAFF,
COLONEL J.F. COLLIER, MEET VON FRANKE AT 500
KILOMETRES

THE LAST PHASE. THE COMMANDER-IN-CHIEF, GENERAL BOTHA, RE-
CEIVES AN OVATION FROM HIS BODYGUARD AFTER DISBANDING THEM

GENERALS BOTHA AND SMUTS, THE GREAT SOUTH AFRICANS, RECEIVE
A TREMENDOUS OVATION FROM THE CROWD AT THE CAPITAL ON THE
SUCCESSFUL CONCLUSION OF THE REBELLION AND THE CAMPAIGN

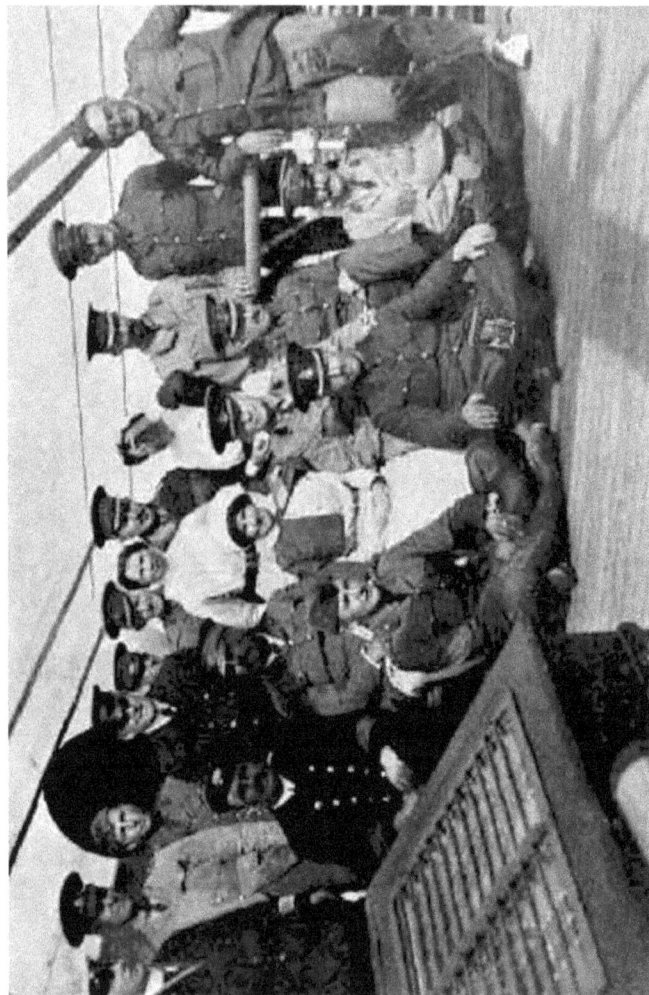

HOMEWARD BOUND! GENERAL BOTHA AND STAFF RETURNING ON THE *EBARI*

THE GREAT MAN AND THE CHIPS OF THE OLD
BLOCK RETURNING TO THE UNION AFTER CONQUEST

With Botha's Army in the
Imperial Light Horse

Contents

The Occupation of Luderitzbucht   111

The Real Thing   119

Sandstorms and Ceremonies   127

Sights and Smells   135

Alarums and Excursions   148

A Night Ride, and After   159

Big Game, But Small Bags   169

War's Grim Jests and Morals   175

Prime Minister's Office,
Cape Town,
24th November, 1915.

Dear Mr. Robinson—

I have not had time to read through the proofs of your book *With Botha's Army*, but a hurried perusal thereof has given me much pleasure. It contains an able and good description of the fine spirit which animated our army in German South-West Africa, and of the good humour which kept our men cheerful under most trying conditions.

I have pleasure in recommending your book to the public,

Yours faithfully

Chapter 1

The Occupation of Luderitzbucht

The story of the campaign of German South-West Africa is written, plain for all time, across the sands of that amazing country, and an empty bully-beef tin, half-buried in the flank of a tawny sand-dune, is eloquent of most of its detail.

But this, of course, we did not know when, on the 11th of September, 1914, we packed our horses on the s.s. *Monarch*, and ourselves aboard the *Gaika* to await the dice-throw of Chance. It is true that we were more or less certain as to our destination, but it is equally true that our knowledge on this point was strictly unofficial, and therefore sinful.

Not that we greatly cared, however. Our optimism was a thing colossal. We were going to finish the German South-West campaign in three months; we would spend Christmas in Cape Town, and by the New Year we would be on our way to a state entry into Berlin. It is small wonder, then, if we felt almost casually patriotic as we ploughed past Robben Island in the wake of H.M.S. *Astraea*, our escort.

The Portuguese explorers, who first discovered the place which held our destiny, called it Angra Pequena; the Germans, who came later, rechristened it Luderitzbucht; and we, who were a portion of a brigade or a fraction of a division—we never knew which!—learned subsequently to know it by a number of other names, most of them inspired, and all of them utterly unprintable.

Incidentally, we were a squadron of the Imperial Light Horse, which had been weaned—too early, some thought—from its mother-regiment, and which now, some five days adrift upon a venture of the waters, sucked at the fingers of Rumour, and stared uneasily at a dim coastline upheaved above the rim of troubled waters. Uneasily, because the "rolling *veld*" (*vide* the English Press), whence we had come, had in nowise prepared us for the rolling ocean, and the waters had not dealt kindly with us. In truth we were a very sick ship, and I am inclined to believe that some amongst us looked upon that sudden appearance of land, less as the attainment of our objective—for it was German South-West Africa—than as a violent and sympathetic upheaval on the part of the ocean itself.

At any time a terrible thing, sea-sickness becomes invested with a horrid grandeur when you may see, as I have seen, whole squadrons and battalions laying their all before their Maker. A great leveller, though. Pride of new-got stars and pomp of crowns and stripes bow before it, and a mere private with sea-legs is worth a dozen brigadiers without. With us, however, there were very few distinctions. The Armoury Guard, posted in the evil-smelling hold, were sick as they presented arms, and the visiting orderly officer succumbed as unaffectedly as he returned their salute.

Thus, for five and a half days, we voyaged—save the mark! We spent the better part of two days balancing ourselves to the thrust of cross-seas, while tugs bellowed around us, and the *Astraea*, or so we understood it, disappeared in search of a German South-West Africa of which our navigators had lost all reckoning—and at the end of that grisly time the tall spike of a lighthouse stood out upon a black fang of rock and a white snarl of broken water, and we were told that it was Luderitzbucht.

There was magic in that intimation. Men who had not been sufficiently interested in things even to accept a chance-sent whisky-and-soda—these were the very worst cases—suddenly busied themselves in cleaning neglected rifles, and even, when they thought that no one was looking, in surreptitious feelings of the points of their bayonets.

Ah! Little did we know then of what was to follow. But the bayonets did come in useful for opening tins of milk, anyway!

After the lighthouse came what appeared to be a land-locked arm of the sea. That slid astern of us, and was followed by a more or less well-defined bay that ended abruptly in a conglomeration of tin and plaster, and red and green roofs. Luderitzbucht beyond any shadow of doubt! What exactly we expected I do not know. It seemed feasible that the place might be fortified and we braced ourselves.

Nothing seemed to happen, however. The *Astraea* dropped anchor at a quarter of a mile or so nearer the town, and that was all. The Reuter man, who used to write what we afterwards learned to call the *Luderitzbucht Society Notes*, would doubtless have said that she trained her guns on the town. Perhaps she did. To us she merely looked supremely bored.

From one or two of the houses white flags that looked like tablecloths were hysterically waving. It was distinctly flattering, and I know that we felt immensely forbearing. Then someone saw the German flag that flaunted its garish challenge to us from the lighthouse, and we began to feel then as a German must, I think, when he ceases to be a German and becomes a Hun.

We landed at four o'clock in the afternoon. It was a very quiet affair. The few inhabitants who were to be seen about tried to look as if they hadn't noticed us, although we rather more than filled Luderitzbucht, and the Transvaal Scottish are a *little* obtrusive at times. There were a lot of ladies, however—ladies who did not look like ordinary inhabitants, and who stood on the verandas of the houses and smiled kindly at us. We blushed by battalions and passed on.

We, the I.L.H., were assigned to quarters in what was called the *"Diamenten Gesellschaft."* When we got there it was dark, and we made ourselves as comfortable as we could—those of us that were not on guard—in a sort of donkey *kraal*. There were some fowls there, I remember, and we performed some quite creditable atrocities with our bayonets. Then—I never quite knew how started the whisper that grew and was flung from man to man and from troop to troop until the whole squadron knew it—*"Beer!"*

Beer. Yes! Dozens upon dozens of cases of it. Long, beautifully long bottles of pale, cool-looking Pilsener. The least said about it the better. Indeed, recollection is apt to be a little hazy upon the point. But this I know, that until the Headquarter Staff discovered that in tackling German South-West they had tackled an uncommonly thirsty proposition, and sent down wagons and took it away from us, every man of us looked at war, if not through rose-coloured spectacles exactly, at least through gold-tinted glasses.

Months later that same beer was retailed back to us by Supreme Authority at ninepence the bottle! Why ninepence? we often wondered.

The first really distinct phase of the campaign was camels. They—there were three of them—wandered in one day out of the desert and were captured by the Rand Light Infantry. Captured! Yes! I think that is the word. The R.L.I., however, seemed vastly more impressed than were the camels.

There is no authentic record of how, eventually, the camels came to us, but we believe it was something after this manner:

> Scene: Company of R.L.I, seen vaguely through sandstorm. More vaguely still, three camels looming out of nowhere in particular.
>
> Company Colour-Sergeant to Company Officer: "Beggin' y'r pardon, sir! But about them three 'ummin' birds ——"
>
> Company Officer: Good God, man! How the devil should I know? Do I look as if I? Oh, damn it! Send 'em up to Headquarters."
>
> Follows period filled in by more sandstorm, grunts of camels, and hearty British cheers, as news flies around that R.L.I, have routed entire German Camel Corps. Then—
>
> Brigade-Major to Brigadier: "Ahem! Sir! Three camels have just turned up——"
>
> Brigadier (absently): Ah"
>
> B,: "What? *The devil!*"
>
> B.-M.: "No, sir! Camels, sir!"
>
> B.: "Camels! Good God! Where from?"
>
> B.-M,: "They didn't say, sir! What are we to do with them, sir?"
>
> B.: "Do with them? Um! Well—er, let me see. Um! Er! Oh! Confound it! give 'em to the I.L.H.!"

So we got them. And, until some eight months later, when the squadron left Luderitzbucht for Walvis, we kept them.

There was nothing very lovable about them. They bit us and they sneered at us, they frightened our horses and they smelt abominably. But they aroused the envy and the admiring interest of all the other regiments, and the nurses used to come up from the hospital to take photographs of them, and so—we kept them.

I omitted to mention the fact that the camels brought a native with them.

Nominally, no doubt, he was in charge of them, but I do not think that he ever let the camels know it. He came to us as well, and he told us their names and a lot of other interesting facts. He said, for instance, that if you ejaculated "Hut!" and kicked them at the same time, they might go—"might," in this instance, was right!—and that if you said "*riwa!*" with the same accompaniments they would get up.

They did, with a disconcerting suddenness that generally caught you as you were half way into the saddle. A word that sounded something like "Twitts," he further informed us, was the signal for them to sit down.

One of our corporals who was looked up to as an authority upon camels, because in his infancy he had ridden one at the zoo, was placed in charge of them, and on the morning following their advent he and the writer and one of our lieutenants took them out—save the mark! they took us for a saunter round the town. We had a good deal of fun that morning, but I think the camels had more. Two of our party, I know, enjoyed themselves hugely when "Landsman"—he was the second biggest camel—tried to rub the corporal off his back against some particularly atrocious German architecture.

To our great joy—the camels were behaving themselves for the moment—we met the whole of the Brigade Staff out for an airing, and, as might be expected of three camels in a very narrow street, attracted their attention.

For what happened to him after that our lieutenant himself was solely responsible. He was explaining to the most gorgeous-looking staff officer exactly how one dealt with camels. "You see," he said, "when you want them to sit down you simply say 'Tootsie.'" (This was quite safe: they were already sitting down.) "And when you want them to get up you just lift your leg—like this—and you say '*Riw*—'"

He had scarcely got the quotation mark out of his mouth when the vast bulk of the camel beneath him rose with the awful suddenness of an exploding mine and smote him violently aloft. How he managed to retain some sort of a hold I do not pretend to know. In civilian life he is a dentist, and perhaps that partly explains it.

Anyway, the rest of that morning's ride is lost in the memory of that lieutenant-man hanging head downwards—his arms clasped around the camel's forelegs, and saying, in all sorts of voices of agonised protest and cajolery: "Tootsie! Oh, d—— you! Tootsie!"

It is not altogether easy to understand why war should be so much more impressive to the spectator at a distance than to the man engaged in it. Perhaps it is that the sense of personal detachment shows things in a clearer perspective, or perhaps, again, it is simply that the terseness of official cablegrams leaves so much to the imagination. Myself, I incline to the latter; but this I know: that the bulletins—we in German South-West were never exalted to the rank of the *communiqué*—which told the world of "the occupation of Luderitzbucht" conveyed a vastly more dramatic aspect of that feat than ever entered the philosophy of those who were merely responsible for it.

For us, indeed, those first few days in Luderitzbucht held more of humour than anything else. Our horses did not come ashore until September 21st—three days after our own landing—and, deprived thus of our sole justification, we loafed around the town or indulged in foraging expeditions as the fancy took us. With the infantry, of course, it was far otherwise, and we were constantly being reminded of the war by the sight of them scuffling away at their trenches and blockhouses.

One of the features of Luderitzbucht was the number of its gramophones. Every house had one. I use the word "had" advisedly, because there followed a period—happily brief—when nearly every one of us included a gramophone in his personal luggage. We did not—indeed, we did not—loot them. We only borrowed them. Which, it may be said, is a difference with at least an air of distinction!

A squadron of gramophones, all playing at the same time, and all, of course, playing different airs—from eternal Wagner to the German equivalent for Harry Lauder—is a fearsome thing, and it is not, perhaps, to be wondered at that they quickly palled. The first note of their decline in popularity was struck, I think, when one night a voice was heard entreating any one—he did not care who—to swap him "a tin of milk for a gramophone, records and all!"

It was at about this time, too, that a brain wave on the part of some staff officer took the tangible form of what were known by the courtesy title of "surprise alarms," and the manner of them was thus: A message would be sent from Brigade Headquarters to officers commanding units to the effect that an alarm would be sounded that night. "The hour for the alarm," the message would add, "is left to the discretion of officers commanding." The utmost secrecy, too, was to be observed, as it was essential that the men should be taken completely by surprise.

The officer commanding unit would then, in the strictest confidence, of course, tell each one of his troop officers, and they, again in the strictest confidence, would inform their troop sergeants; from the troop sergeants it would filter through to the corporals, and the corporals would hand it on to the troops themselves. There, at least, the confidence was justified. The secret could go no farther.

Thus, when a "surprise alarm" did occur, its chief feature, in so far as we were concerned, lay in the well-simulated astonishment of our

O.C. at the extraordinary rapidity with which his men had turned out. Upon one occasion, however, he did most unfeignedly break down. An alarm had sounded. We were in our places, and "the old man" was about to address us in a few well-chosen words, when, to the surprise of nearly everybody, the throaty strains of *"Deutschland Ueber Alles"* fell upon our astounded ears. The culprit, it was discovered, was a man in No. 1 troop, and his subsequent explanation to the effect that the gramophone was a cheap German patent that went off like an alarm clock was, I am glad to say, received with some considerable coldness.

Nearly everyone must be familiar with the fable of Æsop that tells of the untimely death of a herd-boy who played at alarms, of how his comrades wearied in time of the game, and of how one day, when cause for real alarm came, they took no notice of his cries for help, and he perished, and everybody turned round to everybody else and said, "I told you so!"

History, with us, very, very nearly repeated itself. Not, of course, that we should necessarily have perished. On the contrary, we should, in all probability, have gained an imperishable fame.

There had been a succession of these surprises, and when one night we were aroused without having been warned beforehand we were mightily disgruntled thereat, and by way of expressing our disgust, turned out as we had slept—the plutocrats and the more successful looters in pyjamas, and the others in absurdly inadequate shirts. Over these we had, of course, slipped our greatcoats and bandoliers, so that, in the darkness, we looked quite presentably warlike. Then, to our collective horror, we learned that this was no surprise alarm, that something had happened, or was going to happen, and for some quarter of an hour we stood in our blushing *deshabille*, and prayed fervently that there would be no order to saddle up. There was no order, and we went back to our blankets, chastened and deeply thankful.

No power of imagination can conjure up any approach to the mental picture of the squadron of us flaunting our indecency over the mocking sand-dunes for a day or more—as we might so easily have had to do. Even the enemy's camel corps would have blushed the blush of outraged *"kultur!"*

Our horses were landed on the afternoon of the 21st. Poor beasts! Draggle-tailed, cut, and kicked about, they looked like ghosts of the animals that we had shipped at Cape Town only ten days before. If we had suffered to some extent on that memorable trip, what had they, packed like sardines in the noisome hold of a dilapidated sea-tramp!

By the evening, however, hard grooming and ointment had worked wonders, and when, on the following morning, we led them down to the sea for exercise, they bore but little resemblance to the spectres of the day before. On the next day again they had picked up so wonderfully that we saddled up and exercised them. Gentle work at first; but on the 24th, when, for the first time, we mounted in "marching order," they looked fit for any amount of hard work. They got it—sooner than was expected!

CHAPTER 2

The Real Thing

On the afternoon of the 25th the order came that we were to fall in at eight o'clock that night in heavy marching order, and with one day's rations each for horse and man. What did it mean? Was it the real thing at last? Questions elicited nothing. Our officers merely replied that they did not know—there was an order from Headquarters, and that was all.

So we waited, and an hour before the time saw us ready to the last little detail of filled water-bottles and rolled greatcoats. Eight o'clock came, and we fell in with our led horses and waited again.

"Sixty extra rounds of ammunition to each man!" The order came from somewhere out of the darkness, and one could feel the stir of relieved tension as its import went home to the waiting ranks. This was no foolery of surprise alarm! We were going somewhere to do something, and the confused murmur broke into open jubilation. "Stop that talking!" A silence, then the same even-toned voice went on: "There is to be no talking—whatsoever! There is to be no smoking; any man caught striking a match will be dealt with—promptly!" Silence again, broken by the uneasy creaking of leather and the restlessness of horses. Someone was counting in a low voice: "Three, four"—I could just catch the words—"five, six. That's your lot!" and there followed the whispered acknowledgment of the man on my left as he slipped the packets of extra rounds into his wallets. My turn next, and then the turn of the man on my right, and so on, down the line.

"Charge your magazines with five rounds apiece." It was our troop officer who was speaking. A pause, then: "Ready?. ... Prepare to mount. Mount!" Followed a confused jumble as the lines of troops broke and surged and swayed and surged back again. Horses do not like night work, and are sometimes emphatic in expressing themselves.

119

Someone was in difficulties just in front of me. There was a sound of furious bucking, followed by a smothered oath and a thud as the rider landed squarely on his back. Someone else—I do not know who he was beyond the fact that he stood on the ground and was shaking me by the hand—said: "Goodbye, old man. Good luck!" and—"By sections from the right.. ..Walk march!" and he had dodged out of the way of the wheeling sections and was gone.

With No. 1 Troop in the advance—they were to pay, and dearly, for that pride of place before we returned!—we filed off, troop by troop and section by section, into the waiting darkness.

It may in all truth be a small thing, this starting on a night patrol, but it must be remembered that to most of us it was the first taste of anything of the nature. None of us had any conception of where we were going, or why. The country was utterly unknown to us—we hoped vaguely that some one with us knew something. It was dark. There were presumably some German gentlemen waiting somewhere to receive us. We were half choked by a fine white dust that hung about our path, and it was—oh! the greatest fun.

Past the jail we rode, past the cemetery with its white mist of head-stones, past the R.L.I, pickets, who turned out in amazement at the dust-curtained quarter of a mile of horses and men; past the flanks of great granite hills, and so into the open, where the ghostly, half-light—it is never really dark in the sand-belts of G.S.W.—rioted with the imagination and made of sand-dunes mountains, and of mountains clouds that changed while you watched them into belts of trees where no trees could be, or disappeared altogether if you turned from them for a moment, and all the time the sound of our progress went up like the sound of a sea. Always it was with us, that muffled beat of hoofs, that was like the quiet lisp of summer seas as we ploughed through the sand, and the thunder of heavy surf as the squadron took the bare granite.

Hour after hour we rode. No one knew the time, or greatly cared. A blanket of sea-mist came after, and wrapped us in its wet folds, whilst, ahead, a dull red glow in the heart of the darkness set us guessing at our objective. We had seen that same glow from Luderitzbucht on the previous evening, and had been told that the Germans were burning railway construction works at Kolmanskuppe. "A night attack!" The thought tingled, and we rode on, keenly expectant, and as keenly conscious, now, that we were making a good deal of noise, and of what that might mean to us.

With the hours died that half-formed hope. We were too wet and sleepy and cold to care much what happened, and when, somewhere towards the dawn, the order came to dismount and ring our horses, we obeyed almost automatically. ("Ringing" horses consists in tying them, head to head, in a circle. In the ring thus formed the guard has every horse's head within easy reach of his hand, and one man may thus easily manage twenty or even thirty horses.)

This was done as well as our numbed fingers permitted, and we lay down to the most cheerless vigil I ever remember. The sea-mist had gone, and its place was filled by a wind that sobbed over the dunes, and scourged us with whiplash sand, and we lay and burrowed under each other for warmth, and swore for the sake of the further warmth that we might get out of the swearing.

"Saddle up!" Never was order so welcome, and we sat up to stare through sand-rimmed eyes at a dawn, steel-grey and pitilessly cold, but dawn for all that, and by the time that we had worked the stiffness and numbness out of ourselves sufficiently to be able to tighten the girths of our horses (one does not "offsaddle" when the enemy are presumed to be within a few hundred yards of one's bivouac), red day, like a bloodshot eye, was staring over a horizon of lilac-tinted sand-dunes, and we mounted and rode away into a riot of colour that grew more madly drunken with the light.

It is perhaps in some subconscious feeling that one is within reasonable distance of suddenly and violently attaining the ultimate end of things that there lies this fuller and keener appreciation of beauty than one knows at other times. Whatever the reason, however, it is there. I have felt it, and—I have watched others.

Sunrise found us in a world of amazing sand-dunes, and the silence and wonder of the place gripped us and held us. We watched great chunks of yellow and red sunlight flung from dune to dune, caught and held an instant on some bluff crest; then it was gone, and the sand that it had touched put on morning robes of violet and mauve, and dunes farther on caught up the sun's vagrant glory and held it aloft and mocked aloud, and became grey and dead in their turn. Sheer witchcraft! Permission to smoke was given, and the magic of the place took the blue film that rose from the squadron and twisted that into beauty. Farther distances uplifted themselves to colour-drunken senses; fields of alabaster, rose-suffused and laced with faintest blue veinwork. Hills beyond, quivering with unnameable colour and—Hullo! What was this?

The squadron had halted and we could see men of the leading troops dismounting and creeping up the flank of a sand-dune. How slowly they moved. *Bang!*

The shot seemed to come from nowhere in particular, and nothing much seemed to happen, save perhaps that my horse jumped even more violently than did its rider. Who had fired? And why? I looked round at the man on my right for an answer, and found that he was looking at me.

Bang! This time it was undoubtedly one of our own men firing, for I distinctly saw the "kick-up" of his rifle. But at what? *Bang! Bang! Bang!* They were at merrily enough now. Two troops, at least, down to it on the top of the sand-hill. A man, some twenty yards to my left front, shouted something about getting under cover, and the top of a baby sand-dune, about midway between us, was smitten into fine dust by a something that whined as it went on, and we "got"—hurriedly!

Another ricochet cried overhead as we reached the cover of the sand-hill. One troop only was standing to its horses. The others were clustered thickly along the ridge. It was our troop that was "standing to," but no one seemed to be taking any particular notice of us, so we surreptiously handed over our horses and crawled up into the firing line.

Some four hundred yards away was a conglomeration of tin sheds and a small brick-built house.

"What's up?" I asked of a man who was recharging his magazine.

"Don't know," he replied laconically. "*I'm* chipping brickwork! Hullo! One of our chaps has got it!"

A man in No. 1 Troop had slid a few feet down the slope and was holding his wrist. The blood was just beginning to trickle through between his fingers. A cigarette, I noticed, was still in his mouth.

"Only a scratch!" observed the laconic one. "But I wonder where they're firing from. They're not in the house, I swear!"

"There they go!" The shout was raised by someone at the far end of the line, and away down the valley, beyond the buildings, there appeared four figures on horseback, galloping all they knew.

"Nine hundred yards" snapped the man next to me as he readjusted his sights. Everyone was firing now, and the sand was kicking up in little spurts all round the flying figures.

At fifteen hundred yards we gave it up, and a bend in the valley took the four from our sight.

Suddenly there appeared in the wake of the Germans a crowd of running figures, and the firing, which had died down, broke out anew. "Don't shoot! "someone shouted. "They're niggers!" and we held and waited. They were niggers, as we found when, half an hour later. No. 4 Troop had rounded them up—and pretty badly scared niggers at that. They seemed, however, after the manner of the African native, to be in nowise astonished at our not shooting them out of hand; though we learned subsequently that they had most emphatically expected to be destroyed—the Germans had told them so.

It was easy, when we reached the buildings, to learn how the Germans had eluded us with such perfect ease. Behind the tin sheds—one of them bore in large black letters the information that this was "Fort Grasplatz"—the ground sloped steeply to the valley below, and the sand showed us where their horses had been held for them until they had considered it was time to go.

It was all rather humiliating. If we had done this, or had not done that—we grew rather heated over the discussion—we should have got them. Very annoying! but we found some considerable measure of consolation in a breakfast of looted coffee, fancy biscuits, and Limburger cheese. There were some excellent cigars, too, in one of the sheds, and when, eventually we mounted and rode away along the line (Grasplatz, in times of peace, was a railway-station), We felt quite large-minded on the subject.

Our officers, too, must have felt the humanising influence, for we learned from them, in snatches here and there, some of "the reasons why" of our expedition, and out of these snatches we pieced together a fairly consecutive whole. Our main objective, that of bagging the Germans at Grasplatz, had failed—we learned that. What actually we had accomplished was a big loop around Kolmanskuppe, and we were now returning to that place to meet the R.L.I., who had left Luderitzbucht some hours after us on the previous evening. We might see some fun on the way back, but it was very unlikely. That was all.

The railway line which we were following lies along the back of an immense outcrop of granite. To our left, at some miles distance, was the sea; to our right, the desert.

It was worth watching, that desert. Ghostly mirage stalked there, and little yellow sandstorms got up and scurried around among the dunes, and tried to hide the feet of the big purple hills of the distance. The sun was pleasantly warm on the high ground where we rode; we had had the nicest, politest little brush with the enemy,—no one had been really hurt on either side—and now we were going home.

No 1 Troop, still in the advance, was covering the ground to our right front in extended formation. How queer they looked—men and horses seeming at that distance not much bigger than ants!

What the deuce were they up to, anyway? Some of them on the extreme right of the line had turned in and were galloping furiously. Idiots! working tired horses in that way! They ought to be—*Bang!* Good Lord! again? *Bang! Bang!* How strangely the shots sounded, muffled and unreal.

But they were real. Look!

One of the galloping horses had collapsed suddenly, and lay kicking. Its rider picked himself up, ran forward a few paces, and flung down again. The troops on the railway line halted automatically.

A whistle blew and No. 3, just ahead of us, trotted off in a cloud of sand. No. 2 picked up a signal from somewhere, and moved off the line to the left. Still we waited, torn with impatience. Ah! A mounted figure rode out of the press of horsemen ahead. Followed the sound of a whistle, faintly heard, and our turn, had come.

What a breathless scurry that was to where the "old man" was superintending affairs with his very best parade manner. I can see him now, one hand thrust deep into a breeches pocket, a pipe clamped firmly in the angle of his jaw, and that damned enigmatical smile of his, half hid by the drooping moustache. I know, should he chance to read these lines, that he will forgive the adjective. Many phrases that are not included in the vocabulary of nice, polite people are some- times used by common soldiers as terms of endearment, and anyway, his smile was—enigmatical. When he praised—occasions so rare as to be almost negligible—it was there. And it was there when he blamed, which, not unnaturally perhaps, he often did. When, as at the present, the squadron was under fire, the smile grew almost animated.

"Number four!"—the old man used to drawl his words of com- mand as though he liked the sound of them—"number four, action ri-ight!" We were down and were handing our reins to the horse- leaders before he had got rid of the order.

"This way, men!" Our troop officer was scrambling down the slope in the direction of the firing, and we plunged after, charging our mag- azines as we ran.

"There they are!" Two horsemen were galloping obliquely, across our front at about eight hundred yards range. They were unmistakably Germans, and we flung ourselves down and opened fire. At the third shot, fired I think by a sergeant who was sitting down to it a few yards to my right, one of the figures collapsed forward on to his horse's neck, but recovered and hung on somehow, and at about eleven hundred yards they disappeared behind the shoulder of a sand-hill.

The sound of an occasional shot still came up to us from the sand below, but the "fun" must be nearly finished, for No. 3 Troop, on the rocks above and behind us, had ceased fire. They knew, could see, what was going on, whilst we, who were within a hundred yards of what must have been, to judge by the number of shots we had heard, quite a brisk little scrap, could see absolutely nothing. We scrambled on, hoping desperately that everything was not yet over.

We were on the fringe of the sand now, and were beginning to see things. A man—I recognized him as belonging to No. 1—was there, walking aimlessly about. He was hatless, he had no rifle, and he limped as he moved. A few yards beyond him was his horse, and from where it lay a yard-wide spoor of blood ran down to the sand-hills, a full hundred yards away. "Mind the chap in the sand!" It was the hatless one who was shouting. "Oh, mind the chap in the sand!" There were several men "in the sand." As far as I could see they looked perfectly harmless.

One of them was lying flat on his back, with his legs and arms grotesquely out-flung, and as I looked there occurred a phenomenon. From behind him there uprose a third hand and arm that waved frantically for some moments and then stopped and seemed to wait. Nothing happened, and the rest of the man that belonged to the spare hand and arm rose to his feet and stood with both arms upheld above his head—our first prisoner. Ah, well! The "fun" was over now, and we could turn and reckon up the cost.

At the edge of the granite lay a man—one of our men—shot through the heart. Another man was kneeling over him, his head down to the other's breast as if listening for sound of life. With one hand he had commenced to loosen the other's collar; in the other he held, loosely, the strap of a water-bottle. They were brothers, these two men, and—they were both dead. Another—mortally and hideously hurt—was holding his wound with both hands. He was calling out too, I remember. A fourth was being carried up towards the railway line. His leg was shattered at a few inches above the knee, and as he passed he made some joking allusion to his "rotten luck"—he was the man wounded earlier in the morning at Grasplatz. Twenty minutes later they came down and told us that he, too, was dead.

One of the few kind things of war is the little time given to one to think. There are, of course, memories that one carries away—memories of men writhing in agony; of men whom one had known and liked making bestial noises while they died; of horses shattered and maimed, and looking pitifully bewildered in their pain. But the pictures are mercifully vague, blurred. The brain, at such times, is too drunken with excitement to do more than record the bare facts.

And of the remainder of that day, my memory can tell me no more than that, at some hour after dark, we got back to Luderitzbucht, that it rained for some time (a fact unforgettable of G. S. W.); that some of the R.L.I, came up from somewhere .and helped us to bury the Germans; and—that is about all. But stay! There is one other picture that is clear—that of a dark-moustached, debonair man lying propped up against a rock; blood mostly as to the breeches of him (he was shot through the thigh), and utter unconcernedness as to all the rest of him, from his cheery smile to the cigarette that he airily waved to illustrate some point or other to the man who was bandaging him. This was Captain De Meillon, Chief of the Intelligence. His grave is somewhere out there in the desert (he was shot dead some months later near the Aus Nek), and our easy task it is to keep his memory green; easy because—well! he was a fine soldier, but a finer friend.

CHAPTER 3

Sandstorms and Ceremonies

The burial-ground at Luderitzbucht affords striking testimony of Teutonic thoroughness. An area of some three hundred square yards in extent, it contains within its neat boundaries both cemetery and town rubbish-heap.

True, the cinder and empty tin half is quite distinctly marked off from the headstone half—the "God's Acre" of a grim Lutheran humour—but, and it was not alone the suggested "ptomanic" connection between the two "departments" that influenced us, we objected, strongly, and perhaps not unnaturally, when, on the day after the fight at Grasplatz, we were told to carry our dead there.

It is not an aggressively cheerful place. One can picture the spirit of the Fatherland doing the goose-step over it, spurred heel gritting alternately in mounds of refuse and on tombstone, saying: "Here— here we dump our waste material!"

"Better," we argued, "to let our men lie where they have fallen!" but convention, and a desire on the part of some commanding officer or other to ease himself of a neat tribute to our "gallantry," prevailed, and our first casualties lie now in mixed company.

We buried them on the afternoon of September 27th, and the whole of the Central Force came down to see us do it. We formed a hollow square around the graves. To the left of us were the R.L.I., and from somewhere in the murk of sandstorm in front of us the pipes of the Transvaal Scottish wailed dirgefully. "A sandstorm with a stomach-ache," some one called it, but we were grateful, all the same, for their help. To an outsider the scene would doubtless have been impressive to a degree. The sandstorm, the silent mass of khaki-clad troops surrounding the white-surpliced figure that droned of ashes and dust and was inaudible because ashes and dust choked the air into which he spoke, and because his surplice stood out behind him and cracked loudly in the grip of the buffeting wind; the black, cumbersome German coffins, the Lutheran pastor who stood quietly behind awaiting his turn to bury the German dead—we gave them a military funeral, too—and the sobbing of the bagpipes.

Yes, it must have been impressive, but to us, who were so near to things, it all seemed vaguely unreal. They had died too quickly, these men, for us to altogether realise their going. C——'s name had been called out on roll-call that afternoon to attend the funeral parade, and C—— was there—in that long black box with the brass plates and flowered handles. It was all very uncomfortable and disillusioning, and we were more than glad when the last spadeful of earth had been beaten flat and the Scottish pipes awoke and lilted us back to camp on the heels of "Bonnie Dundee."

On the afternoon of the 28th we were ordered to hold ourselves in readiness for another night march to somewhere unknown, and eight o'clock in the evening found us again in the saddle. We knew more what to expect on this occasion. Rumour sprang up and told us that we were going to have another try to bag the "garrison" of Fort Grasplatz, and we were well content that it should be so. We were indebted to the enemy for some few vacancies in our mess, and, only reasonably, we were anxious to settle the little score.

One night ride is very like another. There were the same low-voiced orders, the same doling out of extra rounds of ammunition, the darkness was all-pregnant with just the same vague possibilities.

There was one difference, however. No. 1 Troop, somewhat to their disgust be it said, were second in the order of formation. They had been in the advance on the previous occasion and had suffered, in consequence. It was only fair, therefore, that some other troop should be given the lead. No. 2 took it, and the possibilities, and we moved off into the night.

We did not take the route that we had followed on the night of the 25th. Instead, we struck into the hills, where the squadron clattered over outcrops of bare granite where horses stumbled and men fell, where, at times, we wound in single file around boulder-strewn ridges, or scrambled breathlessly down slopes of rock and sand that were too steeply tilted to ride.

Sometimes—but this was when we had forsaken the noise and clatter of the granite for the velvet silence of the sand-dunes—the section in front of ours would slither away down some unseen slope,

and before we could pull up to consider the position we would ava-
lanche down after them, the horses sliding on their haunches and the
men hanging on somehow and anyhow, or, if they became unseated,
tobogganing on their own. Not infrequently, when the squadron had
safely negotiated one of these slopes, we would look back to discover
one or more mounted figures vainly endeavouring to force their reluctant beasts to hazard the slide. A section in rear would then hand
over their horses, double back to the sand-dunes, scramble up somehow, and then two of the men would link hands under the quarters
of the animal that was refusing the plunge, and, at the instant risk of
being kicked to glory, literally hurl the astonished beast forward and
over the edge.

A low moon hung in the sky, and the dunes stood up in a soft
golden radiance that was caught, here and there, in a gleam of elusive
silver, and, here and there, smudged with inky shade where the flank
of some great sand-hill sloped steeply from the moon's path. Usually,
our guides led us through the valleys of this great dune-field, but not
infrequently, when our further progress was barred by some impasse
of sand, we would take to the higher ground, to the crests of the dunes
themselves, and our path would lie by crumbling lip and over hog-
backed mounds where the white dust rose like a mist around us and
the yielding sand gave knee-deep to our toiling horses.

Heavy work this, and the morrow might see us in desperate need
of fresh horses. The troops ahead of us dismounted in response to
some unheard command and we rolled out of our saddles, glad to ease
the animals and to stretch our legs, cramped with long riding.

For how many miles we walked that night no one is likely to
know, but although that experience was to be the first of many, and
although we got used to it in the end, not one of us is likely to forget
that first weary progress through the dune country. To say that we
were not suitably clad for marching is to put it mildly. In addition to
riding breeches, and leggings, and spurs, over which tired men are apt
to trip, we wore, each one of us, a military greatcoat, two fully loaded
bandoliers (how those buckles hurt!), a filled water-bottle, a mess-tin
that clanked mournfully to every movement, a haversack crammed
with bully beef and ship's biscuits, and a bayonet that usually managed to get in between one's legs at awkward moments; in addition
we carried in one hand a rifle that grew heavier as the slow miles fell
behind, and with the other dragged at the reins of a horse that, being
a horse, could not see the sense of the proceedings, and wanted, every

hundred yards or so, to lie down and rest. When the order came to halt and "ring" our horses for what remained of the night, we were too far gone even to realize our relief. We just threw ourselves down in heaps and slept untidily.

Exhaustion and the bitter cold fought over our bivouac that night, and when grey-footed dawn came shrinking among the sand-hills we were vividly awake, aching in bone and mind.

These things pass, however, and before the order to mount was given we had derived a certain amount of enjoyment out of the performance of our toilet, which consisted of shaking as many pounds of damp sand out of our clothing as was possible without disrobing.

"Get mounted!" The "old man" had ridden past, and his was the mumbled order, the words bitten off as if his jaws were frozen—as they very possibly were.

Some of us, an inconsiderable minority, got into the saddle at the first attempt. The rest found, with a sort of numbed surprise, that sleeping on damp, cold sand is not conducive to that equestrian *élan* upon which, as a squadron, we prided ourselves.

One, G——, notoriously short in the legs, presented an amazing spectacle. He had contrived somehow to get about half-way up the side of his steep horse, and there he hung, like an unhappy limpet, breathing heavily, and trying, apparently, to mesmerize himself into the saddle. Men in happier positions than he strove to comfort him. One unmerciful suggested that he should start all over again, and another recommended the hand-over-hand method of swarming up the stirrup leather as being both safe and picturesque.

A really pitiful sight, too, was our dear old squadron sergeant-major. By virtue of his exalted office he was the owner of the most imposing horse in the squadron, and for the few minutes before a friendly hand canted him up into the saddle from behind, the old gentleman, who was not as young as his attestation papers showed, and was, besides, nearly doubled up with cramp, looked as if he were going to break down, and, as our amateur Irishman said to me afterwards: "Not a blissed handkerchief among the whole squadron iv us!"

Our horses, poor beasts, were trembling with cold, but they moved off briskly enough, as if glad of the exercise, and by the time that we had struggled into some sort of formation they were going quite easily.

Our bivouac, although we had not known it, had lain on the very fringe of the dune-field, and a few hundred yards brought us out on to a hog-backed ridge of granite that to our right uplifted into larger hills, and to our left dipped down into a hollow on the farther side of which stood the block-house of our previous acquaintance.

We gasped with surprise, but there was no mistaking it. There, on the rusted corrugated iron, were the sprawling letters. We spelt them out to make sure: "F-o-r-t G-r-a-s-p-l-a-t-z." On that moment of swift joy, there came an order, back-flung from somewhere in the advance, and we wheeled sharply to the right. We ploughed through a "*vlei*" of white sand. Another order—it sounded like a bark—and we tumbled out of our saddles and crawled, filled with an unholy joy, to a fringe of rocks, and waited.

The squadron went straight on, the "old man" riding a little to one side and in advance. We saw him signal, and watched breathlessly the miracle of precision that followed. No. 2 Troop wheeled half-right, No. 1 three-quarters left. No. 3 swept straight on. They were within a few hundred yards of the blockhouse now. Surely they would be seen! No 1! A hollow in the ground took them, and we breathed again.

Where were the others? No. 2 we could see. The men were dismounting and creeping up the flank of a ridge of rock. No. 1 had disappeared as completely as though they had never been, and we could only conjecture that they were somewhere in the piled rocks to the left of the blockhouse. Hullo! There was No. 3 again, on the sky-line, and far beyond the "fort." The "old man" knew what he was doing, by Jove! Fort Grasplatz now lay in the centre of the squadron, and we snuggled down and blew specks of sand from the breeches of our rifles.

Our troop officer came and lay down beside me with a happy little sigh.

"They won't get away from us this time," he said, and focused his glasses on the buildings.

Below the crest upon which we lay the torn and twisted metals of the railway flung a new note of colour into the lavish scheme of sunrise. Teutonic thoroughness again! Every single section of rail was broken, the twisted ends sticking grotesquely up into the air, and below each a hollow in the sand showed where the dynamite had been placed.

We did not know then what that railway was to mean to us: of the months of waiting that were to be ours, while the engineers relaid the line and pushed it, bit by bit, painfully, farther into the desert; of the blockhouses that were to spring up beside its reconstructed length;

and of the weary vigil that was to be the portion of the infantry throughout that campaign of thirst and blistering sandstorm.

For the moment all our ambition and interest in life was centred in that group of tin sheds across the hollow, and already we began to sense that ours had been a fool's errand; that "Fort Grasplatz" had not been reoccupied by the enemy, and that, after all, there was to be no "fun."

Two minutes later we were sure. A crouching figure appeared for an instant among the rocks on the farther side of the fort, and was gone again so quickly that it seemed like a trick of the eyesight. Another, and then another, and there, below the sheds, a group of three or four more.

"Don't fire! They're our fellows." The warning was unnecessary. In that clear light it was possible not only to see that they were our men, but also, in some cases, to recognise individuals.

"Look! There's old M——." (M—— was a sergeant of No. 3, notable chiefly, perhaps, for his dignity of manner.) At that distance, and on all fours behind a rock, he looked amazingly like a rabbit, and an infectious giggle from somewhere down the ridge was caught up by the line, and enlarged into open laughter.

A few seconds later M—— was seen to be on his feet, making desperate efforts in the wake of a rush of men on the blockhouse. We saw them coerce the door with a rifle-butt, saw one man hoisted by a companion through an open window, and watched while what looked like a pair of boots was thrown out. Followed a shower of miscellaneous articles impossible to distinguish, and our officer rose to his feet, with the light of battle in his eyes. "Loot!" he observed shortly. "Get mounted!"

There is not much more to be said of our second attack on Fort Grasplatz. A note in my diary sums up the affair into the words, "Breakfasted on the remains of our previous loot," and that was really all that happened.

Our first month or six weeks in the German South-West saw several such "attacks," and we used to draw up programmes that told how "on October ——D Squadron, I.L.H., will recapture Fort Grasplatz, under the management of Lieut.-Col. D—lds—n. All bioscope rights reserved!"

The "old man" really did seem to develop an amazing affection for surrounding those empty sheds. We, of course, used to humour him, and nothing could have exceeded the gravity with which we would, time after time, follow him through a night march in pursuit of his hobby, nor surpassed the spirit with which we used to storm the fort under his benign approval.

On this occasion, however, the game was still delightfully new, and if we grumbled at all, it was mainly because No. 3 Troop had collared a case of tinned milk, and had omitted to share it round. It was in things of this kind that the war was brought home to us.

On our way back to Luderitzbucht we rode across the fringe of sand where the Germans had ambushed our advance screen only three days before. Of that brisk little encounter we had carried away a very vivid picture, and we were morbidly curious to see again the festoon of dead horses and to point out to each other where So-and-so had fallen, and where this or that German had lain.

Here was the spur of rock beside which E—— had crouched while he shot the German who had shot his horse, and here, round this corner—Hullo! Where were the horses, and—but this could not be the place, surely? And yet, and yet these were unmistakably the rocks behind which the enemy had lain in wait for us. Then what in the name of all that was wonderful was this sea of sand-dunes doing here? Three days before this had been a level plain of white sand and now——

We rode on, silent with wonder. No. 2 Troop, a hundred yards or so in the advance, halted, and we could see that the head of every man was turned to the right. They were staring curiously at something that we could not see, and we crowded in on the heels of their horses., Ah! So that was the explanation. From the flank of the straggling sand-dunes before us there protruded the quarters and stiffly outstretched hind legs of a horse.

A breeze that was to grow later into a *pukka* sandstorm was driving a fine mist of sand over the crest of the dune, and while we watched a steady, ceaseless stream of sand slid gently down its flank, and quite perceptibly added to the grave of the poor animal beneath. A week later, when we again visited the place, a contrary wind had sent the dunes back whence they had come, and the sun-dried, shrunken bodies of the horses blistered the landscape, plain for all to see.

Wander-dunen of the Germans, ye are fitly named indeed. In that grim desert land, where is neither beast nor bird, your wind-sown graves perform at least a vagrant office over poor carrion that lies by the way—grisly milestones that mark man's conquest of desert and of fellowman—carrion untended else, till, bleached and dried by wind and sun, it moves to the lightest touch, and, finally, is broken up and frayed to dust and follows after the restless, changing winds, leaving only a pile of gleaming bones to mark the spot.

CHAPTER 4

Sights and Smells

The week that followed upon our second taking of Fort Grasplatz brought us a passing interest in new arrivals: the Natal Carbineers, the Pretoria Regiment, the Kaffrarian Rifles, a battery of the Natal Field Artillery, the Eastern Rifles, the 1st Kimberley Regiment, and—it was whispered—a brand-new brigadier with a brand-new staff to match.

A bare note in my diary states simply that they came. Of the order of their coming is no mention, but then, not even official records, I believe, could have lucidly sustained the sandstorm that snarled over Luderitzbucht throughout the whole of that infernal week. Through it were caught glimpses, here and there, of herds of baggage-laden infantry being driven to allotted camping-grounds; of spick-and-span *Carbineers* striving desperately to maintain the dignity of their spurs—and almost succeeding; of kicking mules and cursing drivers; strings of horses, wagons, guns, more drivers (still cursing), native scouts, poultice-wallopers (courtesy title of the S.A.M.C), and all the ragtag and bobtail of our amateur army.

A hard-bitten company of the Veterinary Corps drifted down upon us, and asked if there was beer: they had heard——. We told them. Yes; there was beer, but there was none now. We were sorry. Whereupon, and without enthusiasm, they said that it didn't matter, and drifted away, still searching. Others, but these were of the infantry, forlorn units blown from all knowledge of their whereabouts, we found huddled under the lee of buildings. They bleated at us joylessly, and asked many questions. Was this a sandstorm? Were there many Germans about? and—but this was inevitable and unvaried—had we found many diamonds?

We would usually tell them that our kitbags could hold no more, whereupon they would break down and beg to be taken back to their regiments. We did not, of course, entertain the slightest knowledge of their regiments' whereabouts, but, as something was obviously expected of us, we would indicate variously all four points of the compass, and they would thank us effusively and merge away, one by one, into the muffled landscape.

Sandstorms, however, do not last for ever, and there came at last a day when the unchanged hills looked down upon neat acres of canvas and a new and startling activity. All of our immediate world was become a geometric pattern. Wagons, scores upon scores of them, stood axle to axle in a faultless precision that led the eye along ruled lines to ordered rows of water-carts and tethered mules. A group of these last had broken loose, and half a dozen mathematicians with long-handled whips were chasing them back into equational order. Beyond, again, right-angled horse lines and a crisscross pattern of tents which was the Natal *Carbineers'* camp played with the Natal Field Artillery's 15-pounders at being an Euclidic proposition. Which, of course, was absurd.

It has somewhere been said that an army represents the only true democracy. This is not true. Nowhere is there so nice a class distinction as in the army, and nowhere, perhaps, is that nicety; so candidly maintained. We, the LL.H., would not at that time have even dreamed of visiting the infantry,, but we called upon the *carbineers* because, simply, they were "mounted men," and as such our equals. Later, months later, out of the common thirst and the sandstorms—all men are alike in a sandstorm—there grew the reluctant conviction that active service brings to pass a sort of socialistic millennium in which regiments are judged only by their performances, and in which officers may at times speak quite respectfully to their men, and men almost respectfully of their officers. That the *moral* of the mounted man is usually superior to that of the "foot-slogger" may be attributed solely to the superior *moral* of the horse that he rides. This last is an epigram, but true.

The Natal Field Artillery, too, were on our visiting list, and we found them to be excellent fellows. We swapped lies with them; we pronounced their guns to be the loot of some museum:—they were not, certainly, of the newest type—and we greedily borrowed all the newspapers that they had brought with them.

It was in the N.F.A. lines, by. the way, one white-hot noon, that I almost tripped over the super-philosopher. He was Irish, which perhaps makes his philosophy the less remarkable, and he sate upon an upturned soap-box and toyed with a dish of something that sounded like camp stew.

There was a sudden noise, the sort of noise that makes a grownup say to a child: "You should put your hand before your mouth when you do that!" and I heard, rather than saw, the super-philosopher clear his mouth of some objectionable morsel. I looked round, and his pale eye closed with mine. "Praise th' saints!" he said, "thim ants have no bones into thim!"

Our interest in the arrivals did not last long. A new sandstorm blew up and swallowed them, and when, weeks later, it spat them out again, they had all but lost their identity as far as we were concerned. The infantry became known to us simply as "foot-sloggers"; the *carbineers*, from a weakness for polishing their riding-boots, became "the Cherry Blossom Brigade"; and we, the I.L.H., were known to all and sundry as the "Illicit Liquor Hunters." I do not think, however, that we should have minded so much if there had been any liquor left to hunt.

We were kept hard at work, too, and we soon learned that the "in-betweens" were more profitably, to be spent in what we called "blanket-drill," and what our N.C.O.'s, when they were not indulging in it themselves, called "darned laziness," than in afternoon calls upon strangers who had so thoroughly taken upon themselves the colour of their surroundings as to have become as supremely uninteresting as ourselves.

The deep groaning noise that a trumpet makes at dawn, and which field-officers and poets call "*réveillé*," and turn over again and snore at, when, by some rare chance, they hear it, was to us the first note in a symphony of labour that was to last all day. Who has heard the howls of execration that uprise from a sleeping camp at its first note will appreciate the truth of what I say. The utter hopelessness of any resistance to its summons is, perhaps, what galls most. Turn you never so deaf an ear, you will still have the chilling conviction that some N.C.O., with more liver than bowels of compassion, is waiting "outside" to mark you down as an absentee from roll-call.

Réveillé, roll-call, arms inspection, morning stables, alleged breakfast, stable fatigue, mounted squadron drill, watering and feeding horses, and musketry instruction took us by gentle stages as far as lunchtime. After lunch (save the mark! but is sand, disguised as Irish stew, lunch?), Swedish drill, sectional skirmishing on foot, and an odd quartermaster's fatigue or so thrown in, would lead us on to evening stables. That accomplished, we were at liberty—those, at least, of us who were not on guard for the night—to prepare our evening meal and to retire to our blankets, where, masters of ourselves at last, we could—the writer certainly did on one occasion—dream that one-eyed camels of malevolent aspect chased us through interminable leagues of sandstorm, and finally drove us into seas of greasy Irish stew, wherefrom emerged horrid shapes that lectured us on the care of rifles and the virtues of discipline.

How we longed for war, if only for its comparative peace!

Not all our days were grey days, however. There came a period when each morning saw us, clad mainly in pipes and towels, taking our horses down to a landlocked arm of the sea, where the hills stood up in their glory around us, and where flamingos, in their stately phalanxes, waded the still shallows or flung in broad-pinioned ease to some further sand-hank; where black seals bobbed greeting to us from the dipping waters, and where we could forget the sandstorms of yesterday and tomorrow.

Horses, we found, made excellent diving boards, and lent themselves, besides, to a type of chariot-racing that I have not met elsewhere. For this form of sport it is essential to have two horses, and it usually became one's painful duty, therefore, to borrow the mount of some other man, preferably a non-swimmer, when he was not looking, and then to make for deep water—where he could not follow—with as little delay as possible. Remained then only to so contrive oneself as to stand with a foot on the back of each animal, and to keep them swimming sufficiently near together to allow one to retain some sort of balance. Sometimes one would succeed, but usually, and in spite of extreme efforts, the contrary beasts would swim more and more widely apart, until overtaxed powers of doing the splits would end in a ducking as ignominious as inevitable.

I remember an occasion when, after a long and tiring patrol, we had ridden our horses into the shallows to cool their legs, a school of ground-sharks suddenly appeared, almost literally, under their very noses. The White Knight in *Alice in Wonderland*, who made his horse wear spiked anklets against the danger of shark-bite, must have foreseen some such contingency; but then, had he been with us, he would have fallen off, I feel sure, in the smother of spray and panic which the experience cost us.

One of our duties at this time was the providing of an escort to the water ration that left Luderitzbucht each morning for Kolmanskoppe.

The water was taken in mule-drawn trolleys along the railway line

138

(we possessed no other "rolling stock" at that time) and as it was the sole supply of the two infantry regiments stationed there, extreme care had to be taken to prevent its being intercepted by a stray German patrol.

On October 7 No. 3 Troop had supplied the convoy, and we, whose turn it was to do so on the morrow, had spent the greater part of the day, in the sweet frame of mind that is bred by camp fatigues, and at four o'clock in the afternoon were waiting for the order to "break away" from a squadron drill that seemed as if it would never end. The other troops had dismissed long ago, and we asked ourselves with some bitterness why we should be kept out in the heat and sand playing at circuses, and all the while the sharp words of command stabbed through the curtain of dust that followed us, and punctuated our grumbling. "On the left fo-orm troop!" Someone, hand-jostled by a section in rear, cursed aloud, and we laughed as we went forward at the picturesque phrase he had used. "Sections right!" The sand-fog rose more thickly about us. Was this farce never going to end? "Ha-alt!" Ah! This was the order for which we had been waiting. The "dismiss" would follow, and there was still time if we hurried for a bathe before evening stables.

But our O.C. had apparently forgotten us. He was gazing with something of an air of abstraction at a solitary horseman making towards us from the direction of the camp.

There was nothing really extraordinary in the sight of that figure (we could recognize him, by the big, upstanding grey that he rode, as the colonel's orderly), yet something—his obvious hurry perhaps—made us forget our anxiety to be dismissed.

A minute later he had pulled up before our troop leader. "Colonel D——n's compliments, sir! and you are to report to him at once!" And then, in the confidential tone that orderlies learn from their constant association with the higher ranks: "Water guard, sir!" I could just catch the words: ". . . German patrol. . . one. . . chap wounded. . . . What's that, sir? . . . Yes, one of our fellows."

"Sections right! Wa-alk 'arch! Tr-r-ot!" There was life in the order this time, and there was life, too, in our quick response. The horses even seemed to be infected, and we had to hold them a little as we pounded along in the wake of the news-bringer.

"Steady, there! Ye don't want to ride the sentries down, do ye?" The camp buildings had leaped out at us from the yellow haze of our own progress, and the corporal of the guard had flattened himself against a wall—just in time. We pulled up and rode in soberly. Men of other troops dashed at us and held our horses. "Lucky devils!" they said, and bade us get our *bandoliers* and rifles. From them we learned that a German patrol had lain in wait for the water convoy at a point some three miles up the line, had potted one of our men through the thigh, and had retired without our fellows being able to fire a shot in exchange, and now, we—"lucky 4," they called us—were going out to hunt them. "And I don't suppose they've gone far," one informed me. "I expect they'll be waiting for you, an' p'raps they'll shoot one of you. I know I hope they will—you lucky, lucky devils"

Into the press of chaff and counter-chaff, and the excitement of straps and buckles, rode one, speaking with the large voice of small authority, and hung about with "the complete campaigner's outfit." Not a detail—if we except the camp-stretcher and the cork-mattress—was missing. Water-bottle, haversack, prismatic compass, field-glasses, first aid outfit, and sand goggles—the White Knight again!

As a quick-change artist he should have commanded our ready admiration. As it was, he provided just that sobering touch of humour that we needed. "Go in' to take all week to get ready?" he queried with that heavy urbanity which N.C.O.'s and stage managers mistake for satire, ". . . *passel o' ladies' maids!*"

"Oh! you—you May queen!" I heard someone say, and the troop giggled helplessly as we swung into our saddles. "Number off from the right!" the order was barked at us.

"One"—"two"—"three"——. The fourth man was having trouble with his pony and was far too busy to think of mere numbers, and the White Knight glared down the line of us as if, in some way, just outside his comprehension, we were all to blame. "As you were!" he snapped—it sounded like "Zwear!" "Number off from the ri——"

"No time for that now, Sergeant!" spoke the crisp voice of the O.C. from somewhere behind us. "Sections left! Walk march! Tr-r-ot!" and the quick dust rose to the forward surge of horses and men, and we were off.

Five minutes later we had passed the outlying pickets of the Transvaal Scottish, and were kicking up the sand at a good hand-canter along the hill-girt railway line to Kolmanskuppe. There is a peculiar exhilaration in this form of sport (I cannot easily use the term "warfare "in regard to a game wherein all that is ordinarily known as "patriotism" is swallowed up and lost in a wholesome, primal, man's desire to hunt man—the royalest of royal game—for the sake, only, of the game's lust), and if in G.S.W. we were rather like the famous American hunter who had never been known to kill anything, but who "just hunted"—well, such little killing as did come our way proved conclusively that "just hunting" held all the breathless joy of the thing and left no—aftertaste.

For some miles we held our pace, and the heavy, springless sand through which we rode flung its yellow veil about us. There was the sound of wind in our ears, and the creaking of saddle-leather, a vague surging noise, as of a heavy groundswell sucking through rocks, and, over all, the choking, blinding pall of dust. An oath, back-flung from a leading section where a horse had stumbled, sounded smothered and unreal. Now and again an outcrop of bare granite would leap out to meet us, and the brief thunder of our passing would shout back from the echoing hills; then sand again, and its muffled tumult.

The valley became narrower, and a hint of coolness stole down the sudden shadows. All on a moment a swift hand plucked the sunlight from us, and the jaws of the hills closed suddenly about our path—closed, closed, until the ribbon of steel that we knew to be the railway line looked like a tongue lolling from the cleft grin before us. There was a silence in that place, and our horses pricked quick, apprehensive ears to it.

"What a place for an ambush!" said someone of my section, and the angry "Don't be a fool!" of the man to whom he had spoken showed that three of us, at least, were thinking of the same thing. The click of a steel-shod hoof striking against stone, and—"*click*!" back would come the answer of the rocks; just the sort of noise that the bolt of a Mauser rifle makes when it is drawn back to—— Well, speaking personally, I do not suppose that I should have noticed it if my horse hadn't jumped so.

It was here, or hereabouts, that our patrol had been fired on only a few hours before, and we had received no particular assurance that ours was not likely to be a similar experience. On the contrary, every breathing instant was pregnant with possibility, and, be it said, a sort of half-shrinking hope.

A barrier of great boulders, through which the line won a bare clearance, stood suddenly up against us. Just the place for an ambush; but nothing happened save, perhaps, that one was conscious more of one's own breathing after it was passed. A hundred yards or so farther on the hills to our right fell away in a great curve, and sheeted sunlight lay on all the place; orange, streaked with silver of drift-sand on the shining plain, while beyond, and high above all, white-faced crags swam on an opal-hearted mist. To our right a mad sunset flared above the purple-footed hills, and pointed long, scorn-fill, shadow-fingers at us. Sunset? or drunken magic? Saffron there was, and duck's-egg green lying on amber; amber that dripped molten gold, and tipped with splendid colour the peaks which stood up blackly against it; amber, shot with blush-rose and slashed with fierce scarlet: a breathless wonder that changed while we watched it—changed and deepened until all the painted sky was a blood-clotted glory.

Night had stepped into the valley in which we rode, and I was not sorry when my section was picked out for "flanking work," and we were sent at a sharp trot to the foot-hills and the sunlight. We were told to keep slightly in advance of the troop, and, as the broken nature of the ground allowed, about three hundred yards distant from the railway line, the idea being, of course, that should an enemy patrol be waiting for us among the rocks, we—"the advance screen"—would draw their fire, and so secure some measure of safety for our main body. A leading section was sent off to the shadow-land on the right of the line, and, looking back when we had ridden some hundred yards or so, I saw two other sections detach themselves from the main body, and drop back, to the right and left respectively, as a sort of extended rear-guard.

"As the nature of the ground allowed!"

The words were the letter of our instructions; the exclamation mark, as *Punch* might say, was ours when the first gentle slope that we negotiated jumped suddenly up into a hog-backed "*krantz*," that looked as if it might strain even a klipspringer. It had to be done, however, and we laid ourselves on our horses' necks and let them go at it. What a breathless scramble it was! Loose shale avalanched about us, and steel-shod hoofs slipped and struck, and struck and slipped again on the crisp granite, and just when it seemed to me that nothing was left but to dismount and pull my horse up after me, there was a last, furious straining of willing muscles, a plunge that shook my hat over my eyes, and the four of us were landed in a hard-breathing bunch on a sort of shelf of rock. A girth had slipped, and we paused while it was tightened, and looked back. The troop was halted—while we attained our position, I supposed—and as we watched, a figure rode clear of the others and signalled agitatedly to us to advance.

It was comparatively easy, from our elevation, to select a route that conformed measurably to our instructions and to the opposing factor of our own instinct of self-preservation. Only comparatively easy, however, because distances that looked flat, or, at the most, but gently tilted, proved on closer inspection to be almost worth the serious consideration of an Alpine Club. But we managed to scramble along somehow. When possible, we even went farther into the spirit of our instructions, and rode in extended formation, but, although our horses displayed an amazing aptitude for rockwork, we usually found ourselves progressing in single file.

Once, I remember, when a flat surface of rock tempted us to something approaching a trot, we pulled up only a few yards short of where the hill ended abruptly, and lay, piled about its own foot, hundreds of feet below. It was from there, too, that we first caught sight of the white buildings of Kolmanskuppe, some two or three miles away, but although it was a cheering sight, we went on from that place with much sedateness and circumspection. All serious thought of meeting the enemy patrol had vanished, of course, with that first glimpse of "civilization." Only one ordeal now remained: to get ourselves down, out of that region of sunlight and breathlessness, to where, with the lesser hills, began the last phase of our journey.

One attempt landed us in a *cul-de-sac* of tumbled granite, another on a tongue of rock that would have proved perfectly negotiable if the tongue had not been bitten short, or if there had been a bridge across the forty-foot chasm that grinned up at us; but, eventually, by winding in single file round a spur of rock where a false step meant—as one of us said and giggled so much at, that he all but put his assertion to the proof—"more than a bad cold" for the man who slipped, we found a steep slope wheredown we tobogganed with safety and some amusement to ourselves, but not a little detriment, I think, to the tails of our horses.

The troop, we found, had taken courage of the less imposing scenery, and were just visible in a cloud of dust some half a mile ahead of us. Just outside Kolmanskuppe the railway line takes a sharp bend to the left, and as half a mile in the rear does not exactly correspond with the M.I. handbook's definition of an advance guard's position, we kicked up our tired animals and made a desperate effort, by cutting across the angle of the line, to regain some measure of dignity. What the troop thought when, some ten minutes later, we reappeared in advance of them, I do not know. They looked rather indifferent, I thought, and when, soon afterwards, a ragged fringe of infantry appeared on the sky-line above us—Kolmanskuppe is on the edge of the desert proper, and looks as if it had been washed up by the sea of mountainous sand-dunes—and the troop, realizing apparently that there was really no need to follow its meticulous course along the railway metals, wheeled sharply to the right, we cantered down and, with all humility, tied ourselves on to its tail.

In the number of its houses, Kolmanskuppe is not a large place; in the extent covered by such buildings as there are it is quite considerable. An average distance of about one hundred yards between the houses, and the glaring monotony of their design stifles any desire on the part of the visitor unduly to prolong his tour of inspection.

In the ordinary sense we were not, of course, visitors, and besides, we had "done" Kolmanskuppe, more thoroughly than an American tourist does Rome, on a previous occasion. Then, we had been actuated by other than guide-book motives, and now, its interest gone, the place was become an eyesore, and we wanted to go home. That, we supposed, was why we got the order to off-saddle.

The one picturesque touch in the picture was supplied by our three camels. They were there on some water-carrying pretext, and they recognized us from afar off, and came and stood to windward of us so that there could be no remote possibility of our not recognizing them.

We never seemed, somehow, to be able to get away from those three gaunt beasts. No matter the direction of our journeyings, we always met them sooner or later. We should not, of course, have minded if they had shown any signs of awakening affection for us, but they didn't. It was their sneering indifference to our presence that galled us most, I think. Had we been in the habit of thrusting ourselves upon them, this attitude would have been understandable, even commendable; but we didn't thrust ourselves upon them. They hatched deliberate plots to meet us in unexpected places, and when we met they sneered at us, and besides, as I have said elsewhere, they smelt abominably. In very truth, Tartarin of Tarascon was not more haunted by his own camel than were we by our three.

The corporal who was in charge of them slouched to us from somewhere out of the desert—he was borrowing habits right and left from his camels, we often told him—and gave us the cheerful information that we were to convoy some wagons back to Luderitzbucht, which wagons, he added, were only then being off-loaded. Dusk was spreading like a grey blanket across the face of the sands, and the prospect of a night ride at the tail of a string of creaking wagons was not enticing. We asked him how he knew, and he retired into his newly acquired camelism, and went off to his uncouth beasts.

But he was right, and an hour later saw us—or heard us rather, for it was pitch dark—starting on such a ride as I hope never again to suffer. The road from Kolmanskuppe to Luderitzbucht is rendered distinct from the country through which it runs by means of white-painted paraffin tins placed at irregular intervals along its alleged sides. That it does not otherwise differ to any marked extent from the surrounding country is due less, I think, to the surveyor than to the country, which is mainly precipices and small but very knobby hills. I have since travelled that road in the daytime, and its unrelieved roughness—unless an occasional wallow in deep sand can be called relief—makes of it a thing to be remembered; but of that night, when our nostrils, and our throats, and our eyes were filled with the dust kicked up by close upon a hundred mules and half as many horses, and our ears were deafened by the harsh thunder of empty wagons bouncing into and out of deep holes and over fire-spitting granite boulders, recollection is a mere headache.

For the first half-mile or so—my section had now become the rearguard—we rode at some fifty yards behind the last wagon. We did this for several reasons: firstly, because the air was less full of dust at that distance; secondly, because we could more or less select our own pace instead of having, every now and then, to pull our horses back upon their haunches to avoid spitting them on the brake handle of a wagon stopped suddenly, in its drunken career by, virtue of collision with some more than usually imposing obstruction; and thirdly—but this I do not think was a real reason—because we had been ordered to do so.

We were going down some unseen slope, I remember, when the change occurred. My horse was plunging a good deal, and I had to use both hands to prevent his getting away from me. The man on my right seemed to be having similar difficulty with his animal. Strange! they were all quiet enough a minute ago, and now "Look out!" The words were shot at me by No. 3 of the section as, with his horse completely out of control, he raced passed me into the darkness and the dust. "Rummy," said the man on my right, "I don't know what's the matter with the beasts. They're scared out of their lives, that I'll swear—Good Lord!" His ejaculation was spoken away from me, for his pony had swung suddenly about with a quick, frightened movement, and was now staring into the blackness from whence we had come. A moment later and my own beast had spun around. We waited in silence.

"Where's T——?" said the other man suddenly. (T—— was of my section, and I seemed vaguely to remember that he had been riding behind us.) If my memory was right, then T—— was somewhere out there in the blackness, and the—the—whatever it was that was frightening our horses was out there with him. It was not a nice thought. We waited again, and I found myself wondering what it would sound like to call out T——'s name, when out of the darkness came the sound of a snort, followed by what seemed like the frenzied plunging of some heavy beast. Then a voice uplifted itself in earnest supplication, and the voice was the voice of T——.

He seemed to be calling upon the name of a god not altogether orthodox. I caught, here and there, strong expressions of his disapproval of some person or thing. The voice was growing louder and clearer, and it became obvious that T—— was being borne towards us at a high rate of speed. The pale sheet of the sky held him in silhouette for an instant, and then he flung down upon us in a perfect flood of invective.

I had never heard him talk quite like that before. It was really, and almost literally, illuminating, and we reined aside in a sort of reverential awe to let him pass. He did so on the wings of some of the most golden eloquence that it has ever been my lot to hear. "Goddam!" I heard distinctly, followed by a string of words which I do not know how to spell; and then some fine but strictly censorable phrases, out of which I collected fragments that made a disconnected yet interesting whole. In this I was puzzled for some moments by the many variations of the word camel. "Camel!" I found myself saying, "camel!" when "Look!" said the other man suddenly, and I looked, and saw striding down upon us from the same pale sheet of sky that had held T—— only a few minutes before three gaunt, long-legged shadows.

"The camels!" said the other man, and I looked at him, and he looked at me, and what there was in that shrouding darkness to tell each what the other thought I do not know; but, as our frenzied horses waltzed and plunged away from the acrid fear behind them, we clung to our saddles with both hands, and rocked and choked with insane laughter. Later, when we met T——, leading a dead-lame pony out of the rocks, we broke out afresh, and between paroxysms, told him something of our admiring respect. Indeed, a man who could steer a madly racing pony through pitch darkness and over and between rocks, and at the same time conduct ably a rhetorical discourse

146

on the (presumed) illegitimacy of camels and the moral degeneracy of men who ride upon them, well deserved some more tangible expression of merit than was held in mere words. Iron crosses have been given for less.

The remainder of that ride left to us only recurring fits of laughter, dust, and noise and darkness, and when the camels came too near, which, in spite of concise injunctions to them to go "to another place," they often did, spasms of wrathful and sulphurous abuse.

A note in my diary says of our return to Luderitzbucht:

"Surprised to find myself looking on the beastly place as 'home'!"

But was there real cause for surprise?

CHAPTER 5

Alarums and Excursions

Never, I believe, was there a campaign so casually regarded by an army as was the G.S.W. "affair" by the force that operated from Luderitzbucht.

Even in the first flush of our landing on German territory we looked upon it as merely a stepping-stone to the larger issue in Europe. For that we had volunteered. This was merely an irksome little duty to be performed *en passant*, a sort of preliminary canter to the race into Berlin. We believed that we were going to polish off the local brand of Hun in three or, at most, four months, and then, if we were not too late—and at that time we half feared that we might be—we would join in the scamper across the Rhine, or help to capture the "German High Canal Fleet" from the land.

Some of the more imaginative of us, indeed, went to some pains to draft a sort of Cook's tour of the war. From G.S.W. we would go on to German East Africa. Egypt and the Dardanelles would follow, and then—mere geography being sacrificed on the altar of our splendid optimism—we would enter Galicia from the south-east—or was it the north-west ?—where General Botha would assume supreme command of a mixed force of I.L.H. and Cossacks, whom he would lead through Austria to the inevitable Berlin.

For most of this the corporal who was known as "O.C. Camels" was responsible. Time hung heavily on his hands, and at such odd moments as he could tear himself away from his smellful charges he would come to tell us that he had "just overheard the colonel saying——," or "a ship has just come in, and the chief engineer, whom I knew some years ago at Dar-es-Salaam" (of lavish mendacity was the 'O.C. Camels'), "and he tells me that——." And then would follow some wildly improbable yarn, told with such earnest conviction that at least one-third of the squadron existed in a perpetual state of readiness to join Shackleton's South Pole expedition so as to "go round the other way, and attack the Germans from behind," or to crawl to Windhuk on their hands and knees in the guise of a flock of sand-rats, or something else equally feasible.

At this time our chief grievance against the "authorities" (vague term embracing everything from the mismanagement of sandstorms to the shortage in the rum-issue) was that they never took us into their confidence regarding the conduct of the campaign. We were never told, for instance, when we got the order to "saddle up" whether we were destined for a mere patrol, or whether the long-looked for general advance had at last begun, or whether it was only another "surprise alarm."

One deplorable result of this was that a man might just as easily forget his rifle when starting on an expedition as not. Indeed, we had an example of that on the day that we landed at Luderitzbucht. I had noticed one of our sergeants looking a little more imposing than usual. A sort of forced dignity sat heavily upon him, and I was wondering as to the reason when there came to us an officer, who looked him up and down, as one man of fashion may quiz another who is without his cane or his gloves, or whose trousers are without their customary crease. "Sergeant L——," he said, "where is your rifle?" A flush crept up the sergeant's suntanned neck, and his ears glowed hotly: "Please, sir, I left it on the ship, sir!"

And that on the first day of all! Small wonder, then, that we never, from first to last, learned to regard war as other than a somewhat uncomfortable pastime.

Thus when, on the 4th of October, the smallest of the small hours saw us being coerced from our blankets by the official toe of the corporal of the guard, we merely smothered him under a cloud of profanity, and turned over and tried to get to sleep again. But it was of no avail. He emerged again, pawing his way through the veil of obscenities, blindly, like a man who has been "gassed," and tempted us anew with the news that the Germans were even then surrounding the camp. We listened patiently until he had finished, and then someone told him with a wealth of lurid detail that there weren't any Germans in the country. "There were five originally—and a little yellow dog," the voice went on to say, "but we bagged the five at Grasplatz, and if you think you're going to get me up at this time o' night to chase after a Goddam poodle, you're mistaken!"

I do not know who invented the "little yellow dog." He was always with us. Like the "Brer Rabbit" of the American negroes, he is a fable—the fable of "D" Squadron I.L.H.

But we knew that it was of no use, and within ten minutes we were flinging saddles on our astonished horses. I do not think that we altogether believed the story about the Germans; but while there is any sort of hope there is no "grousing," and it was a moderately contented body of men that rode out into the first paleness of the coming day.

A brief half-hour later we were completely undeceived. Our troop leader halted us at the beginning of the gorge through which runs the railway line to Kolmanskuppe, and told us with a bluntness of speech and a total lack of consideration for our feelings which showed that he, too, regretted his blankets, that we were to "guard the *kopjes* along the railway line." "What for?" I wondered, as I gazed up at the crags that cut blackly into the growing light behind them. As far as I could see, they looked eminently capable of guarding themselves.

"At about nine o'clock," the O.C. went on to say.—it was then about three o'clock, by the way, and most infernally cold—"a water-trolley will pass on its Way to Kolmanskuppe. At about five this evening, it will return. Until then no man is to leave his post, unless dam-well ordered to!"

For this, then, we had forsaken our blankets in the middle of the night; for this we had burdened ourselves with much extra ammunition and tins of bully-beef and jam. "Told you there wasn't a bloomin' German in the —— country!" said the voice that I had heard earlier; but this was when my section was dragging its horses up the scarred, rock-strewn flank of the hill that we were to guard, and the O.C. was away out of earshot, posting other sections on other hills.

There is little to be said of that first day spent on the hills. Recollection blends it confusedly with the memories of many other days spent in a like manner. For the first hour or so, I remember, when the hills swam in the pure light, when the air was good to breathe and tobacco was a God's gift, our watch was pleasant enough; later, when the shade went and the flies came, and the rocks whereon we lay or sat grew so uncomfortably, hot that it was impossible to remain for long in any one position, and the writer even went to the length of pillowing his head on a nosebag and trying to sleep in the shadow of his horse, until the poor, fly-pestered beast tried to dance on him, and he got frightened and ran away; when the landscape rose on its hind-legs and waltzed in the shimmering heat, and our bully-beef resolved itself into a horrid mess of sinew and mystery floating in yellow grease—then the four of us, who liked each other well enough in ordinary circumstances, forbore all conversation, because it was too hot to swear, and sat and shied chips of granite at venturesome black lizards until the shadows came again, and brought with them a hellish discord of shouting and cracking of whips, which was the water-trolleys, and our signal to go home.

It was upon our return to camp on this day that we were told that the R.L.I, pickets had shot two Germans who had attempted to sneak into Luderitzbucht on the previous night, but, generally speaking, the diary which I kept at this time shows in its almost discourteous brevity something of the boredom of manner with which we regarded the campaign in general.

"*October 14-15-16*," an entry reads. "Camp. Sand and flies in equal parts!" An entire page of it is given up to a description of a snake and lizard fight which was witnessed on one of our *kopje*-guarding expeditions, and October 11 is marked down as having been chiefly remarkable for a "stand to arms" that was suffered in the middle of the night because an enthusiastic sentry of the Pretoria Regiment mistook the rising moon for an enemy bonfire or something of the sort, and tried to shoot it.

During the latter half of October it became general knowledge that information was leaking out to the enemy. Certain houses, wherein dwelt Germans "on good behaviour," I know, were being watched. One of these "ticket-of-leave" Huns, I remember, had been retained by the authorities as a sort of sanitary inspector. He was a weird-looking little person with spectacles, and he used to ride about the town on a horse several sizes too large for him. One day, he was gone, and his place was filled by a rumour that told how he had been sent to Cape Town to be executed as a spy. Whether this was true or not I am in no wise prepared to say, but anyway the mere story gave our sentries such a zest for their work that the R.L.I, succeeded on the same night in seriously wounding one of their own officers who was "visiting rounds."

At evening stables on October 17th—a day which only narrowly escaped being bracketed with the "sand and flies" entry of the previous three—we were told to draw our next day's rations in advance, and to see that our water-bottles were filled. Not a word was said to us of any kind of movement toward. "*Ours not to reason why,*" nor even to suspect, and that, I suppose, was why an hour after dark found us with our horses saddled, waiting for the "surprise." We took leave to presume, with that fluent pessimism which marks the really good soldier, that it was going to be another attack on "poor old Fort Grasplatz." (Up to then we had captured that historic place on no fewer than four separate occasions, and we were getting rather tired of it.) But when we were formally paraded, and told that the Natal Carbineers were to accompany us, or rather, seeing that they were the senior regiment, that we were to accompany them, we were quietly uplifted among ourselves, and looked forward to a new venture.

Nor were we altogether disappointed. We were told that our objective was a night march on a place called Elizabethbucht, where was a military post which we were to attack at dawn. From there we were to return in extended formation—with the four squadrons of *carbineers* we would be able to cover a sweep of from ten to twelve miles of ground—to thoroughly "drive" the country back in the direction of Luderitzbucht, and to snap up any German patrols that might be caught in our net. To make things more certain the Transvaal Scottish were going to move out during the night to a distance of some three or four miles, there to await such stray enemy patrols as might be driven on to them.

It all sounded beautifully simple, and although things did not turn out quite as we hoped, without that alluring programme before us we could not, I am sure, have sustained so cheerfully the night's work that was to be ours. It was bitterly cold. A knife-edged wind came and played with us among the rocks wherein we rode, and some time later, when we had forsaken the hills for the easier going of the sea beach (Elizabethbucht, which is some fifteen miles distant from Luderitzbucht, is on the coast), an ice-cold sea mist settled about us and soaked us to the skin. For some five miles we held to the coast, the call of sea birds in our ears and the taste of salt on our lips. Hills grew up again around us, and rocks took the place of sand. All sound else became drowned in the steady snarling of an ebb tide that sucked over some unseen bar, save once, when there came to us from somewhere out of the white-streaked waters a sudden noise of jabbering, like old men in heated argument, and which I now believe was a colony of black seals, but which then, in the darkness and the uncertainty of the night and our mission, sounded mightily uncanny.

At what hour we halted and "ringed" our horses, I cannot say. The sound of the sea was gone, I know, and with it the soaking mist. But

of that bivouac there are two outstanding memories, each as unforgettable in its way. as the other. One was the spectacle, which struck us as
being funny, of *carbineer* officers walking about with stable lanterns in
their hands looking for comfortable places to sleep in, and the other
was of a voice that spoke to me out of the darkness, bidding me to
sleep with him because he was cold, and, when I complied with the
request, of a flask of brandy that was thrust into my hands, with a
whispered injunction not to thank him "quite so loudly, because, you
see, old chap, ours is a very thirsty squadron, and this flask is so little,
so very little!"

Dear old M——! should you chance to read these lines, remember
that if my thanks on that night were not over-effusive, and if, as you
said, I did drink rather more than my fair share of the brandy, at least
my gratitude is of a lasting nature.

We slept, or rather pretended to sleep, under the lee of a big rock,
and there grew up during the night, and stuck into my ribs, a lesser
rock which I tried to uproot, but upon which I broke all my finger-
nails instead, and my stable companion accused me of ingratitude and
of rowelling him with my spurs. Dawn, however, came at last, and the
order to mount: a grey dawn that showed nothing of the coming of
the sun; just a spiritless half-light wherein rocks and sand and men
took on a uniform dull hue. In all that landscape, we found to our
surprise, we were alone save for a squadron of *carbineers.* that was making off at a sharp trot at a wide angle to our own course.

My section was sent ahead to a distance of some four or five hundred yards; flanking sections cut themselves away from the squadron
and galloped out until they were abreast with us and at some hundred
yards range, and we started. For hours, it seemed, we rode, before the
sun's rim stepped out upon the curtain of far hills, and yellow, watery
light quickened our shivering horses. Sand and rocks and scrub—we
were to meet with real vegetation, for the first time, later on—scrub
and sand and rocks—a wilderness that howled aloud.

For slow miles the changeless horizon seemed to mock our
progress. Ridge after ridge of rising ground promised new things and
gave us the same old monotony—rocks and scrub and sand.

It must have been nearly eight o'clock—we had, anyway, for some
time been discussing the breakfast that we were not going to get—
when a sudden dip in the ground brought to our view a collection of
tin shanties and a miscellany of diamond-working plant. The whole
face of the earth was heaped up in mounds of gravel and sand, and be-

tween the mounds were hand-rotators and barrels and quaint-looking cylindrical sieves. The squadron halted while we went forward to investigate. Crowds of pigeons flew about us as I dismounted at the first open door, and went inside to investigate. A half-eaten meal, a glass with the dregs of beer in it, and a bed unslept in. That was all. The second hut told the same story of a hurried departure, and the third, and the next.

"No Germans for us today, my boy!" said the man who had held my horse.

"Never mind the Germans," said another; "I've found a tin of pineapple!"

Half an hour or so later the hoofs of our horses rang sharply on the metals of a narrow-gauge railway line half-buried in the sand, and soon afterwards an official-looking tin roof grew out of the shoulder of a humpbacked sand-dune.

The "military post" which we were to attack! We reined in and looked around. The squadron seemed to be a long way behind, and we were only four; but curiosity is a more impelling factor than mere courage, and within a couple of minutes we were dismounted before a notice-board which told us in official black letters that this was the Elizabethbucht police-station! Some few fowls wandered in and out of the open door, and a brace of pigeons were flirting on the rim of a chimney. Military post! Pshaw! this was worse than Grasplatz! There was a thudding of hoofs behind us, and we looked round to discover the colonel's galloper. "'The old man'," he began, his eyes not on me, but on the doorway of the station—"'the old man' says ye've got to go and find the *carbineers!*"

"Where are they? Are they lost?" I asked, faintly sarcastic.

"I don't know—an' 'the old man' don't know—if they're lost, or if we're lost, but ye've got to go and find 'em."

"But where are they?" I looked away to the barren horizon.

"Don't know, I'm sure," he answered over his shoulder—he had dismounted and was stooping to the low porch of the building—"but 'the old man' says ye're to gallop like th' divil!"

I got into my saddle thoughtfully. Now, where on earth, in a wilderness of sand-dunes and rocks, might one reasonably expect to find *carbineers* growing? They were not behind us, certainly, or we should have seen them. That left three cardinal points of the compass for me to choose from. To the left, and in front, unbroken sand-dunes met the sky in an ugly straight line. To the right, a glimpse of blue sea showed over the crest of some sugar-loaf sand-hills. That, at least, looked friendly, and I started off at a canter through the deep sand.

The *carbineers*, I knew, might just as likely as not be in either of the other two directions that I had discarded, and I might be riding straight into the Germans that we had come all this way to meet. It was on the heels of this thought that I realised, with something of a shock, that I did not particularly want to meet them—just then. A wide valley opened up before me, and I held straight down its centre in some vague hope, I believe, that I might be out of range of the hills on each side. It was not only the thought of the Germans that was bothering me. I might—the day of miracles not yet being past—I might even meet the *carbineers* and they might mistake me for a German, and some of them, I now remembered having heard, were rattling good shots.

Even ordinary peaceable citizens in ordinary peaceable times have been known to remark on the extraordinary resemblances that one sometimes sees in rocks to men and dogs, and even to cattle. On this occasion I saw no dogs or cattle, but I saw dozens of men, all unmistakably Germans, and all in lethal attitudes. Of course they were only rocks, and I kept persuading myself of the fact, but once, I remember, when a prone grey figure that I had been watching for some half-minute or so seemed ever so slightly to change its position, and the next instant I heard a twanging rush through the air above my head, I ducked on to my horse's neck and wondered for a moment where I was hit. On the next instant I looked back to find that a line of telegraph-poles had crossed my path and it was the wind in the low-hung wires that I had heard.

The valley down which I rode opened out into a waste of sand, and I became aware of a string of horsemen moving diagonally across my front. I cantered on for a few hundred yards, and watched them while they halted and faced round in my direction. It was impossible at that distance—fifteen hundred yards at the very least—to tell whether they were *carbineers* or not, and as I moved forward I held out my hat in my right hand. This was the signal by which we were to distinguish friends from foes, and I waited anxiously for its acknowledgment and return. One—two—three hundred yards slipped past, and still they made no sign. Four hundred! This was getting serious, and I reined in to a walk. Five hundred! Ah! there it was! A man had ridden clear of the others, and—blessed sight!—he was giving the "All right" signal.

A few minutes later I was explaining myself to an officer. "Colonel

D——n's compliments, sir!"—and here, since the galloper who had
sent me on that wild ride had not told me what "the old man" wanted
with the *carbineers*, I plunged recklessly—"and will you be so good as
to link up with him, and—and commence the drive."

The end of my speech sounded lame in my own ears, but it
seemed to be what the carbineer officer wanted. "Right!" he said,
"and where precisely, in all this large country, might Colonel D—— n
be found?"

I indicated, vaguely, the desert whence I had come; a whistle blew
shrilly, and the wide-strung line of horsemen wheeled half-right to
the signal that followed, and we moved on again. Far below us, and
to our left, the still waters of Elizabeth's Bay—as the new maps know
it—winked in the sunlight, and a cluster of some half-dozen tin sheds
stood out in clear relief against the white sand of its beach.

Nearer still, and running parallel with our course, was the narrow-
gauge railway that we had met earlier in the morning. A mule-drawn
trolley, guarded by some half-dozen horsemen, provided the only life
in the picture.

"What's that?" I asked of a trooper who was riding next to me.

"Prisoners!" he replied, and, seeing my surprise, added: "Non-
combatants, of course; diamond-diggers, or something. One of 'em's a
woman"—he paused and chuckled. "She came out o' one o' the huts
with a flutter like a lot o' hens when we surrounded 'em this morning,
an'—well, it was very early, y' know, an' old Stick-in-the-mud"—he
indicated an officer who was riding slightly in advance of us—"he
made us right-about while she collected herself." He paused again,
and looked ruminatingly at the officer-man. "I never seen 'im blush
before!" he concluded.

A group of specks appeared on a far ridge. "Are those your fellows?" "Stick-in-the-mud" had called out to me over his shoulder.

"Yes, sir," I answered unhesitatingly, although, as far as I could tell at
that distance, they were just as likely to be Germans. I was right, however, and within a quarter of an hour I was back in my own section.

From this time onward we did not seriously entertain any hope
of meeting the enemy. Too obviously they had received wind of our
coming, and as the affair seemed destined to resolve itself into a picnic—well, we would treat it as a picnic! Thereafter, although we kept
to our extended formation when the nature of the country allowed us
to do so, save once, when the nearness of the sea tempted us from all
semblance of military virtue, and we rode our horses into the breakers,

we treated the whole affair as schoolboys treat a half-holiday.

For an hour or more we rode in the shadow of great hills, or picked a careful way down deep gorges, where bushes—actual bushes, with green leaves on them—brushed our horses' bellies, and clouds of yellow and white butterflies danced mazily away from the disturbance.

Hares were numerous here, and once a species of buck—a rhebok, I think it was —jinked away among the strewn boulders, and once, again, I saw a man dismount to put his heel on the ugly, squat head of a puff-adder.

Somewhere about midday, when, by dint of sheer ingenuity, we had managed to interpose a small ridge of hills between ourselves and the rest of the squadron, my section spread themselves sumptuously over a repast of tinned pineapple and cold tea and bully-beef that was sufficiently melted to be impossible as bully-beef, but just tolerable, when spread on dry ship's biscuit, as a sort of butter.

When eventually we rejoined the squadron, we found that our subterfuge had really been unnecessary, as they, too, had lunched; but then, I do not suppose that we should have enjoyed our meal one half as much if we had eaten it honestly.

During the afternoon the hills disappeared and a field of sand-dunes spread itself across the face of the country and drove us to the easier going of the sea-beach. The *carbineers* had gone from us—we vaguely understood that we were still in touch with them, but where or how we did not greatly care—and we idled along in perfect contentment of mind. Our path was hemmed with beauty on that afternoon. Pink-hued flamingos gemmed the sandbanks; from the rocky islets whereon they drowsed black seals lifted inquisitive snouts to our passing, and now and again our horses would snort uneasily at the bleached skeleton of some immense whale.

Somehow, in G.S.W., landscape follows landscape with the abruptness of stage scenery, and when, suddenly, the coastline curved away from us, a hundred yards or so of heavy progress through a tongue of the dune-field, brought us to a wilderness of small granite hills. As a background to these again were the larger hills, behind which, we knew, was Luderitzbucht.

A nearer sky-line became peopled with specks. One of them was waving a flag, but no one of my section understood the Morse code, and we lost the message. The specks were the signalling section of the Transvaal Scottish, and a quarter of an hour later our horses were snorting and shying at kilted apparitions that arose upon all sides of us from the bare sand.

These, too, were the Transvaal Scottish, and I think that we gained a new respect for them on the spot. That a half-company of men—and I counted at least fifty of them —could lie in the path of a body of mounted troops and remain absolutely undetected until the horses were almost literally on top of them, was a lesson in the practical value of taking cover that is not easy to forget.

"How long have you been lying there?" I asked of one.

"Since about three o'clock this morning," he replied.

I looked at the glowing sunset behind us, and proffered him my tobacco pouch—the only sign of respect within my power at that moment.

CHAPTER 6

A Night Ride, and After

A mile-long tunnel of dust roofed with dim starlight.

That is really all the story of a night ride through the desert lands of German South-West Africa.

There are other things of course: hills that rim the vague earth round, showing like so many dark gaps cut out of the night; the sullen murmur of the sands; the brief outcry of bare rock over-passed; the wheezing of sand-choked horses; but all, muffled sight and muffled sound alike, are just vague impressions sensed rather than seen and heard.

Be your company one thousand men or but one score, you are aware only of those just ahead of you and of some few that follow after. Beyond the range of a murmured curse—and night service in an enemy country does not permit of emphatic blasphemy—is the barrier of dust and night. Only when the way lies over hills, and you may look down and see the dark snake of the column writhe out upon the pale sands below, or watch the constant firefly flicker that tells of stress of steel-shod hoof and naked granite, may you gain the peculiar courage of numbers. When you are in the desert proper, and the white sand lifts its curtain about you, you can be, almost dreadfully, alone.

There are incidents, too. The dismounted group that you pass, bending to the prone figure whose horse, perhaps, has fallen with him; the halt while some unsuspected scout rides in to report what you, gentlemen of the rank and file, will never learn; the low-voiced "Non-commissioned officers!" and the group which forms to listen to orders that you strain your ears to catch; the order to mount, and the undertone of laughter at the plight of some unfortunate whose horse "objects." Forgotten as soon as passed, it will be days before memory can shuffle these happenings into any sort of order, and weeks, some-

159

times, before they can be told.

On October 22nd was just such an experience. We were paraded at dusk, and after the usual harangue on the uncomfortable punishment which would be ours if we talked above a whisper, or so far forgot ourselves as to strike a match, we rode down to the Natal Carbineers' lines, and waited: waited while the men from Natal asserted their regimental seniority and rode away ahead of us; waited while some ambitious water-carts that had got mixed up with the advance were brought back again; waited while a troop of the Rand Intelligence Corps—the "Rest In Comforts" of our own strictly unofficial Army List—were tacked on to the tail of the column; waited while some wagons that had got lost were found; and finally, when patience had worn very thin indeed, were permitted to move off into the dust-choked darkness of another unknown quest.

When hope runs high, things little in themselves assume enormous proportions, and the wagons and water-carts were to us on this occasion what a straw is said to be to a drowning man. And we were drowning, drowning in a sea of despondency. A month of unremitting sandstorm, relieved, if that be the expression, by three or four hopelessly blank expeditions, had reduced us to the condition, almost, of believing that there really were no Germans in the country. And now we were being sent out with water-carts and wagons. We had never had them before; therefore—our logic will not, perhaps be altogether clear to any one who has not experienced similar hopes and fears—therefore there must be Germans at the end of our journey.

Where, before, we had ridden all through the night, only, apparently, for the pleasure of riding back again on the following day, midnight, on this occasion, found us at Kolmanskuppe being guided by drowsy infantry pickets to horse-lines already prepared for us. This in itself was surprising, but the horse-lines were infinitely more so. "'Orse lines?—*bloomin' clothes-lines!*" I heard a scornful voice say. Poles, festooned with slackly hung wires—and these at an average height of about six feet—did, certainly, give to the place the respectable air of a laundry annexe, but they were better than nothing, anyway. We hung up our horses as best we could, and went to sleep in our spurs.

There is an art in sleeping in the sands. We had long since discovered, for instance, that however cold the night, the sand held always something of the sun's warmth, and we used to scoop out hollows to the depth of six inches or so to sleep in. Usually, after half an hour or less, warmth and grace alike would depart from us, and we would be

160

driven to further finger-stubbing searches after warm beds. A wakeful night, indeed, would often present a weird spectacle. Dark forms, heralding their uprising by soft curses, would emerge at intervals from the silent sands around, crawl on hands and knees for some few yards, burrow vigorously for a while, and then drop with a grunt into temporary silence.

I remember one occasion, when I slept with three or four others in a pit of our own digging, and was afterwards profoundly grateful to the bitter cold which had driven us to the expedient. During the night I awoke once or twice to a half-consciousness of a growing wind, and of some weight of sand upon my blankets that was not there when I turned in.

"There'll be a proper sandstorm tomorrow," a sleepy voice had said, and I remembered afterwards how casual had been my agreement.

Dawn, on that morning, came in with a shout. There was a clanging of iron, a sound of devils' anvil play, and, with the realization, the swift onrush of some great thing that loomed upon us out of the sand-haze. I was sitting up trying to clear my eyes of caked sand, but instinct, or something quicker than myself, flung me down, and the same instant was filled with huge sound, and a hint, just a hint—nothing more—of tremendous pressure. When it had passed I sat up again to stare at the retreating form of a cylindrical water-tank which had bowled over us where we lay.

I have no idea of the weight of that tank. It measured, I should say, not less than twelve feet by five, and the wind which was chasing it across the territory was also whirling sand-drift before it at an easy sixty miles an hour. We were considerably impressed, and went to some pains afterwards to measure the inches of our escape. Our "surface-lines," we gathered, must, on the average, have been just about flush with the desert's face. I say "on the average," because one man there was of our party who spent a not inconsiderable portion of the ensuing week in nursing a knee that had omitted to take cover with the rest of him.

The first half-hour or so of that morning presented an amazing spectacle. For the greater part of the time was nothing but sand and the savage wind, but at intervals the booming sound that had first awakened us would herald the passing of other water-tanks. Where they came from I know not, nor can I hazard any guess as to where they were going. They simply loomed out of the sandstorm to come, on the one hand, and were whirled into the yellow fog of sandstorm past, on the other. Later, when we had removed ourselves and such of our belongings as we could find to the comparative shelter of a line of railway trucks, we saw one of these cylinders trundling merrily along at an undreamed of pace.

"Wonder how it's going to take the railway line," someone asked, and we watched breathlessly. At some hundred yards or so short of the line a drift of sand turned it in a sudden, savage curve in our direction, and for fifty yards or so it skated on one screaming rim; but the wind swung it plumb again, and its shrill clamour became a deep grumble. *Crash!* The three-foot bank on which the metals gleamed seemed to jump out to kick the tank high into the air. For an appreciable instant it floated, and then it boomed to earth again, and a fresh wave of sand-storm rose to its impact, and it was gone from us.

Within ten seconds we were making for the spot where it had landed. Arrived there, we looked at each other in silence, and then proceeded solemnly to pace off the distance from the point where it had struck the bank. When we had done so, we remembered the earlier visitor who had stepped over us in the dawn, and we looked at each other again. In that appreciable instant during which the tank, looking like some snub-nosed Zeppelin, had seemed to float in the air, it had covered twenty-seven generous yards.

This has been a long digression, and is only pardonable as being to some extent expressive of the chaos of anecdote which dwells in the mind of the average sand-buffeted sojourner in the desert. Let him loose on one story concerning sandstorms, and he will strip his memory of all the other sandstorms that he has ever seen or heard of to make his one story presentable. Even of myself I can say that I find it safe to write of things that happened in that campaign only when I have my diary propped up before me.

Dawn, then, on that October 23rd to which this chronicle must confine itself, found us half blinded by just such a sandstorm as that which I have described. There was no spectacular display of water-tanks, but the sand-blast was so pitiless that I do not think we should have minded much if the whole of the expeditionary force's rolling-stock had rolled down upon us. We built shelters—that is to say we erected sheets of corrugated iron, borrowed hastily from the buildings on the heights above us, and called them shelters. We built them with their backs to the searching wind, roofed them, and weighted the roofs down with large stones, but some law of vacuum that we never quite got the hang of made whirlwinds in our doorways and drove us finally to the length of swaddling our faces in cloth. The ostrich of the fable, who buried his head in the sand, was not such a fool as our wise men have tried to paint him.

Our horses, poor beasts, turned their backs to the searing blast, and were grateful to the nosebags which we hung upon them, less, I think, for the sake of the grain than for the protection that they afforded to tortured nostrils.

At about five o'clock in the afternoon things began to happen. The sandstorm, after a final furious effort or two, died away as suddenly as it had come up in the dawn; coffee, made in some infantry mess in one of the houses, was brought down to us in great cauldrons; troop sergeants arose and told us to feed "and be —— quick about it!" and when we had stuffed ourselves with army-biscuits soaked in black coffee, a casual-looking train strolled round a bend in the line, and gave us a glimpse of General McKenzie and, along its dingy length, of a fresco of Staff officers and hospital nurses.

Handkerchiefs were fluttering to us, and we suddenly became conscious of the fact that our sand-encrusted state held something of the picturesque. Non-commissioned officers who up till then had been content to stare moodily at the sand suddenly became imbued with huge energy, and stood in heroic postures and shouted meaningless orders at troopers who were too busy "doing their bit" to take any sort of notice, until a real order came from somewhere, and we fell in to listen to instructions.

"Water-bottles to be filled. Rations for horse and man for one day to be drawn. Rifles to be inspected. Greatcoats and blankets to be rolled up—and to be left behind."

"—— to be left behind!" H'm! it was going to be cold work then. But what did the cold matter? What did anything matter? We were not going to travel light for nothing. There was fun ahead. Joy!

We listened in a deep content, and when the order came for us to fall away, we did not wait for any more, but flung upon the quartermaster and demanded things necessary for the welfare of man and beast. We heaped our overcoats and blankets upon him, and contumely when he told us that the rum ration had not arrived.

Not, of course, that we really minded. The rum was of a particularly vile order, but it seemed to represent something that we had left behind us when we "joined the army," and we used to insist upon the issue, and when we had got it, we used to screw up our eyes and drink ostentatious silent toasts.

"Saddle up!"

The welcome command cut short our pretence at grumbling, and we seized saddles and bridles and rushed the horse lines. A quarter of an hour later we were paraded and inspected by the general. The scene, I think, may not have been altogether unimpressive. The dark mass of *carbineers* were paraded in front of us, and the ridge above was black with watching infantry.

The dregs of a sullen, purple sunset brooded over the far hills, and the air, warm and pulseless, was oppressive even after the sandstorm. In any other country one would have said that "it looked like rain," but in that desert the thought even was not admissible. The slow light faded, and the spectators on the ridge became a ragged black fringe.

A knot of these, midway between ourselves and the *carbineers*, raised a faint cheer. What was happening? *Ah!* There was a stir and a rustle among the troops ahead of us, and we could see the dark column writhing out as squadron after squadron linked up and thrust forward. Our turn came, and with it the familiar smell of kicked-up dust.

The same order as before: Natal Carbineers—four squadrons of them—in front; ourselves next; then the Intelligence (why behind? I wondered); and then the dust walls closed upon us, and we—my section, that is, with those immediately before and behind us—were alone.

For some miles we kept to the railway line. Stettin, marked large on the map, but consisting in reality of a tin shed and a signboard, and nothing more—the place memorable where we had first run into the Germans—was passed while there was still sufficient light to see things. There was the spurred heel of rock whence the enemy had ambushed our advance, and there were still the dead horses—dark blots on the grey sand.

Nothing much in themselves, but of deep interest to men who had existed for nearly a month on the bare memory of that first brisk little skirmish among the desolate sand-dunes. A mile or so farther on we passed Fort Grasplatz, looking now pitifully abandoned with its splintered door still swinging on twisted hinges, and the untidy litter before the store which we had rifled for food and drink. It had looked vastly different on that first morning when it had risen out of the sunrise to spit bullets at the ridge whereon we had lain.

Thus far, Grasplatz had represented the farthest point of our wanderings. We had paid several official and entirely uneventful visits to the place, and its attractions had long since palled. From now onwards was brand-new country, and the thought gave to the bare-shouldered hills before us something of a sinister lure.

It was somewhere among these black granite ridges, miles after we had forsaken the railway, that the darkness ahead was split by a sudden flash of white light, and before my horse had ceased to expostulate—on his hind legs—the deep-throated growl of thunder rose above the sound of our progress.

From then onwards, throughout the night, our way was lit by the streaked flame of a storm that seemed never to get any nearer. Unsuspected hills stood up in instant silhouette against the glare, and were gone, and came again, and went. There was not a breath of wind, and the heavy pall of dust choked us as we rode forward. Dead-white walls, whereon each night-stabbing flash painted spots and Catherine-wheels of shifting colour, shut us in, and the dull muttering of the night's wrath swallowed all sound else. The slow miles dropped behind, white sand gave place to red, and then the real darkness came, and with it the smell of rain. The horses smelt it, and one could feel the new life in them as they lifted their heads and opened wide nostrils to its coolth.

But the rain never came. Only the lightning woke the white sparkle of steel in the curtain of fine red dust that rose in swathes about us, and the mocking storm-god growled in his throat at our longing. Somewhere towards the dawn we off-saddled, and laid ourselves down for such sleep as we could find.

On our left hand, and seen only when the vagrant lightning threw its bulk into dark relief against the clouds, towered a red-walled mountain of sand. On the other side of it, somewhere, we understood, was a place marked in capital letters on the map as "Rotkuppes." How far, or how near, we neither knew nor cared. We were too tired to strip ourselves of our bandoliers even, and we lay as we had ridden, hung about with all the uncomfortable accoutrement of the M.I., but it was a happy, thought,, all the same, to know that Rotkuppes was on the farther side of that hill. Capital letters must surely spell Germans, and we were really very, very keen.

A warm wind searched us out at dawn, and we awoke and saddled up under a sky of deep-bellied clouds that looked as if they needed only a push to make them rain. We wanted that rain almost as badly as we wanted the Germans, but in the meantime the *carbineers*, still ahead of us, were on the move, and someone—he might have been our troop officer, or only a sergeant, so sand-obliterated was all his rank—rode swiftly down our lines and bade us hurry. I like to think that he was only a sergeant, though, because his language was not in any sense befitting an officer; but we were mounted and moving off before he had got rid of the half of what he must have wanted to say, and it didn't really matter much, either way.

To our great surprise we had ridden only a few hundred yards when we were ordered to dismount again. The main body of the *carbineers* moved off a hundred yards or so to our left, and halted. One squadron of them handed over its horses, and made for a lip of sand that ran obliquely across our front to the plain below. Others, among them the Intelligence men, were creeping up to the crest of red sandstone that towered up above us. To our right was open desert.

"Look!" said a man suddenly to me, "there's the general." It was true. He was there, kneeling down at the extreme left of the *carbineers* festooning the ridge in front. Captain Botha, his A.D.C., and the son of South Africa's Prime Minister, was with him. Both were staring through field-glasses at something that was hidden from us by the shoulder of the hill, and while we watched I saw the general turn and speak swiftly to his companions. A moment later a *carbineer* officer slipped down from the bank and ran, crouching, in our direction. He was obviously excited, and we watched him curiously. Arrived in the hollow where we stood to our horses, he jerked himself upright, and waved his arms violently in our faces.

For a moment I half feared for his mind, and then I saw that he was looking, not at us, but at the ridge behind, and I turned and saw, silhouetted against the sky, a group of ammunition pack-mules. At all times, as has been sung elsewhere, a mule is a mule, but when he is perched against a skyline, in full view of such of the enemy as may be within a ten-mile radius, he looks, sublimely, an ass. The man in charge of them was obviously interested in the behaviour of the officer in the hollow, for he stared curiously down at us. "Oh! you dam fool! You —— you dam fool! Who the blind blazes sent you up there? Come to h—ll out of it!" I heard the officer-man mutter—he did not dare to shout—but it was of no avail, and the pantomime might have gone on for sometime had not a group of *carbineers* who were lying in cover some fifty yards below the crest scrambled up and awakened the muleteer from his dream, and dragged and pushed his reluctant beasts down the slope and into the hollow.

"Consider yourself under arrest!" The words were barked at the now thoroughly startled-looking custodian of the mules, and the officer turned and bolted like a rabbit back to the ridge.

"'D' Squadron!. . . get mounted!" The order sent a quick thrill down the line, and we lifted briskly to our saddles. "Sections right! Tr-r-ot!" and we were off, swinging for the ridge whereon the *car-bineers* lay. The order came again: "Sections right!" and as we turned a rifle shot cracked in the dry air with the sound of a whip, and on the instant after the entire ridge blazed into a fury of rapid fire. Of the enemy we could see nothing—they were still hidden from us by the sand-wall—nor could we tell if they were firing back or not, although I can remember just how I glanced involuntarily to my right to see if any saddles of my troop were empty.

A few seconds later we were in the open. The firing ceased with that one savage burst, but I do not think that we were conscious of the fact for some time afterwards.

Close under the ridge lay a white horse, its rider sitting up with both hands raised above his head. We were quite close to him, and could see that he looked more astonished than frightened. Some yards beyond these stood another horse, obviously badly wounded—its back humped and its head drooping. A figure in a blood-spattered grey uniform lay untidily beneath it. His right arm, smashed by a bullet, was doubled back from the elbow; the other seemed to be twisted under the body. One foot was still caught in a stirrup-iron, and the upheld leg gave to the whole wretched picture an air of horrid jauntiness that the white face of the wounded man made only more pronounced.

Then occurred the thing that was to make of tragedy (for even killing your enemy may be tragedy) farce. Our farrier-sergeant, a gentleman chiefly notable in that his tongue was as rough as his professional rasp, and whose place was anywhere but where he happened to be—at the head of the squadron—was seen to draw a large pattern army revolver, and charge down upon the stricken German. For a moment we hovered in wonderment at his manoeuvre, but when we saw him rein in, and solemnly present his pistol at the unfortunate man's head, and heard him say, in what his victim must have considered quite unnecessarily loud tones: "Hands up! ye —— blaggard! Hands up! or I'll blow yer —— head through yer chest!" then, then we just collapsed. Our officers, even, forgot themselves and smiled, and we, pit and gallery, non-commissioned officers and men, yelled with laughter—a music-hall *tour de force*.

After that, the third and last group that we saw seemed superfluous, and, besides, both horse and rider were too obviously dead to be of much interest.

I have since come to the conclusion that war is not in any sense a refined pastime.

CHAPTER 7

Big Game, But Small Bags

Somehow, we seemed always to be playing on the outer fringe of war. One fierce little encounter only had there been—a sort of "appetiser" before the dinner that we were never really to taste; since then—nothing! We had stalked blockhouses, surrounded forts, had even hurled ourselves upon military posts; but the blockhouses had invariably proved to be empty, the forts had borne the aspect of abandoned *kafir* stores, and closer inspection had shown the military posts to be, as a rule, more post (usually with a notice-board on the top of it) than military. We suffered gladly the hardships of long night-rides to "destinations unknown," and when, as they invariably did, these expeditions ended in nothing, we made a jest of our curses and hoped for "better luck next time."

But the next time was the same, and the time after, and the time after that; and now after two long nights in the saddle, and a day of pitiless, scourging sand-storm, the great moment had come. "D" Squadron, I.L.H., had been sent out, with the acrid smell of cordite in its nostrils and the cold grip of battle in the pit of its stomach, at full gallop, to "*do or die*" against—three very badly crumpled Germans. It was really too funny.

This was not war. It was some new game of which, as yet, we had not quite got the hang. Gone from that moment were the last lingering shreds of any respect that we might have entertained for the campaign, as a campaign. But what, then, was it, if not a campaign? A picnic? Assuredly not! The hot-breathed sandstorms; the flies; and the water—or, rather, the want of water—denied the term with a brutal emphasis. No! it was a game of sorts, and for myself, I began to have a haunting suspicion that at some time, somewhere, I had been through it all before. Where, then? And how? For the life of me I could not remember.

"Seems pleased with himself," said a voice near me, and I looked and saw General Sir Duncan McKenzie talking to our "old man," and smiling affably. A minute later he left and strolled over to a bunch of *carbineers* standing to their horses at the base of the hill on our left. He chatted to the officer in charge for a few moments, and I could see him pointing towards the desert as though indicating some plan. "There," one could almost hear him saying, "there I will have such and such a troop posted; this squadron will move over there; that squadron will——," and a wave of the arm completed the sentence.

And then I knew. Of course, it was not war, or anything like war. It was a partridge-drive. General McKenzie—his ruddy face, his snow-white moustache, and his general air of business-like geniality making of him the pluperfect country gentleman—was our host. We were the guests; there had already been one drive—not a very successful one— and now we were being assigned to our positions for the next.

Then occurred the thing that was to heighten to an almost absurd degree this appearance of a typical country gentleman directing a typical "shoot." Thus had I seen the thing happen, years before, in an English countryside.

The general had left the *carbineers*, and was walking to some rising ground where he would better be able to overlook the "guns," when he swung suddenly half around, and stood for a moment as if turned to stone. For a moment only; then—and I have some six hundred and odd witnesses to support me, remember—he shook his fist at something or somebody that was hidden from us by the swell of the ground. Then he shook both fists, and then, as if he felt that the display was inadequate, he brought his lower limbs into play and actually danced a few steps. His voice came to us through the clear air, and—but, no! it would not do. He is a general; I was only a corporal, and anyway, it was not swearing; it was pure oratory, of a quality that should have bowed in silent shame and envy the head of any squadron sergeant-major within hearing. A breathless minute passed, and then—or so it seemed to us who were watching—there crawled out of the sand at the G.O.C.'s feet an abject-looking officer-man. Host and blundering under-keeper; they faced one another for a few moments, and then the abject one drifted away on the flood of rhetoric to strand eventually on the sand-ridge behind which lay the three crumpled Germans with their dead horses.

Arrived there, he shook himself and looked over. What he saw seemed on the instant to put new life into him, and he straightened himself and became a fair understudy of the exalted rage behind him. "What the hell d'ye think y'are?" we heard him ask. ". . .. blasted war correspondents? Come out of it, you—you banana-fed tourists!" This was a gibe at the men from Natal, and we chortled hugely among ourselves. A short minute later, when there appeared on the crest beside him a group of unhappy-looking *carbineers* armed with Kodaks that they tried in vain to hide behind their injured expressions, our mirth was helplessly open.

To them came the general. Mounted now, and at the top of his form, one short, *staccato* burst sufficed to place the entire group under arrest. A sweep of his arm seemed to include a troop standing to horses some fifty yards farther on. The troop looked away with immediate ostentation, and the general turned to us. For a moment I thought that he was going to put us under arrest, too. "Colonel D-n-lds-n!" he began, "get your men mounted, and take them—" A wave of his arm indicated the sweep of hills to our right front, and then, as our CO. swung to his saddle and rode forward to meet him, his voice dropped and I could hear only fragments: ". . . spoiled everything!. . . you will. . . . .men. . . ride like the devil!"

Five minutes later we were in the open, dust and the drum-thunder of hoofs upon us, and the song of wind in our ears. "Steady the pace!" a voice shouted, and the troop ahead seemed suddenly to lift back at us out of the sand-haze. For a moment, as we reined in, was a desperate confusion of sections driving through broken sections before them, and of troops as orderless as herds of panic-ridden antelope. A matter of seconds only, and then the broken back of the column mended somehow, and we swept forward again. But the pace was steadier.

It was a day of clouds. A sky, fiercely blue, was burning great holes in the sag-bellied vapour overhead, and the desert's face about us was fungus-blotched with shadow. Miles away to our right the hills that guard Tschaukaib stood up blackly against the white promise of the rain. Upon the knees of the red hills along whose marge we rode was a hint of greenery, and here and there, between the shifting cloud-shadows, the dead-white glare of the open sands below us was tempered with the same soft touch. The miles fled past us. Shadows stood out of the distances, became real hills, sidled past, and were gone. Once, there was a tree —the first we had seen in the country—and the wonder of it held every man of us agape until it became lost in the dust-haze behind.

Shortly afterwards the hills ended abruptly, and a field of sand-dunes, all silver-soft in that soft light, shut us suddenly in. Here was heavy going indeed, but no slackening of pace. The old, familiar curtain of dust rose up about us and hid everything. Through it there came the sudden, shrill blast of a whistle, followed by a sound of struggling. A voice cursed briefly, and someone, or it may have been two or three, laughed. A riderless horse plunged past us. "That's so-and-so's mare," a man in my section said. "Wonder why he's off?" A moment later and he—we, all knew. There was a sudden check in the sections before us—for all the world as though the troop had charged into an immense plum-pudding —and then my horse's hindquarters dropped away from behind me, and his head shot up into the clouds. I clung on grimly, and watched, with a sort of horrified fascination, the straining hindquarters of a perpendicular beast somewhat to my right, and, seemingly, miles above me. The animal was a strawberry roan, and I recognized it as H——'s mount, and I remember, too, that I wondered stupidly where H—— was until my own beast's head and rump resumed their normal horizontal relationship with a jerk that nearly shot me out of the saddle, and I looked up to find a very breathless H—— holding on to the bridle of a strawberry roan as scandalised-looking as himself.

We were on the roof of a sand-dune, and partly for curiosity's sake, and partly to tighten a girth which had slipped, I dismounted to peer over the edge. What the angle was of that steeply tilted wall up which we had ridden I do not know. And even if I did know, I would not write it here because I should not expect to be believed. The slope—call it that if you will—was not an inch short of forty feet, anyway, and it was as steeply tilted as—as a walking-stick; which information, I know, conveys less than nothing, and is therefore the best possible kind of information under the circumstances.

Surprises came quickly after that. The dune-field narrowed until it was less than a hundred yards across, and we became aware of three horsemen—mere specks in the white distance—making in our direction. They could only be Germans, and we rode cheerfully forward to meet them. There was little of order in our going. Some half-dozen men of my troop, separated from us by a gulf of deep sand, rode in a forlorn independence at some one hundred and fifty yards distance, and a group—unassorted—of men from other troops jogged sheepishly behind us, and tried to look as if they belonged. A riderless horse, treading stiff-legged on clouds of disdain, jinked loftily by as though the saddle slewed under its belly were a mark of honoured distinction conferred for the losing of its rider down some wall of sand.

There was a curious lack of excitement about the proceedings. The Germans were hidden from view for a time by a lofty dune that seemed to stand on the shoulders of its fellows. There was plenty of time, however. They were coming in our direction, so what need to hurry? We reined in to a walk, and finally, in response to an order, dismounted and strolled to a lip of sand overlooking the white plain before us. A vast plain it was, ringed about with hills. A distant sky-line was dotted with specks advancing in open formation, and a helio winked restlessly from somewhere on our left front. Nearer at hand, but still at some two thousand yards range, was a small group of horsemen, and from them, as we watched, came a sudden sputter of rifle-fire, but at whom they had fired we could not say. Through field-glasses it was possible to see that one of their horses limped badly as it moved along. Our own three Germans—and it was impossible to avoid a feeling of proprietorship in regard to them as they rode trustingly towards us—were now within some six or seven hundred yards, and the soft "*snick*" of a rifle-bolt pushed home by someone near me struck a note that was all grim.

Nothing—I had almost said the "inevitable nothing"—was to happen, however. At five hundred yards the three caught sight of us, and reined in. For a few brief moments they gazed at us like startled buck, and then their hands went up in token of surrender.

Half an hour later, when we rejoined the *carbineers* at Rutkuppes proper—the capital letters which had meant so much to us spelt, in this case, one dilapidated tin hut and a tarnished name-board—we found that they, too, had bagged a brace and a half of Germans.

Of the three, one was a heavy-faced man of middle age; another, a little person with round shoulders and heavy gold-rimmed spectacles, looked like a student. (We learned afterwards that he had been a chemist's assistant in Luderitzbucht.) The third was a pleasant-looking boy of about nineteen. All three wore the corduroy uniform of the reservist, and looked vastly different to the scouting party which, at Stettin on September the 25th, had stood up to the squadron of us until they were all shot down with one exception, and that exception had only surrendered when his rifle was empty. I felt rather sorry for these men. With the exception, perhaps, of the boy of nineteen, they looked cowed and miserable. The little fellow with the gold-rimmed glasses was trembling violently—we were told afterwards that his hands had had to be forcibly pulled down, so anxious was he to emphasize the completeness of his surrender—and the heavy-faced man was twisting and untwisting his fingers, and he muttered occasionally to himself. An interesting sight even if a little nauseating.

Surrounding the prisoners was a dense crowd of *carbineers*, and out of their gaping regard arose the touch of inevitable humour that marked everything that was said, or done, or thought, in that pantomime campaign. Through the silence of deep interest that held the crowd came an awestruck whisper. "Golly!" it said. "What fierce-looking brutes!"

CHAPTER 8

War's Grim Jests and Morals

"We sat down in the sand and played auction bridge, and the people at home called it 'war'!"

This, the least flattering, and certainly the briefest description of our campaign that I have so far heard, was said to me by a man of my squadron whom I met in Cape Town months after the word "German" had been wiped off the map of South-Western Africa. It is true that in earlier sketches I have emphasised the fact that we did little more in G.S.W.A. than play with war; but to call it auction bridge—well! to every man his own especial type of reminiscences, and perhaps—who can say?—the embittered one may have held bad cards.

The gambler (I cannot for the moment recall the less emphatic expression) may remember chiefly the strange conditions under which he has revoked; your real, hardened citizen, on the other hand, may look back with a mild or wild surprise—the degree of his astonishment depending, of course, upon the degree of his hardness—to the outstanding fact that he learned in the desert to look upon mere water as a precious beverage; the mind of the small despot will dwell, to the exclusion of almost everything else, upon the corporal's or sergeant's stripes that were his, or upon the "favouritism"—a word dear to the patriot under arms—that kept him undecorated; while for myself I can say that by few things in that campaign of hard-edged ennui was I more impressed in the end than by the truth of art oil-painting which I saw in Luderitzbucht within a day or so of our landing.

A man, dying of thirst, blood-red as to the colour of him, and hideous hate and suffering as to all else of him, was lying upon a vivid orange sand-dune, and cursing with his eyes, and mouth, and feeble, outstretched arm a blue, smiling sea—the water that was of no use to him—that mocked at him from across a beach of purple-streaked white sand. The woman who showed me the picture informed me that it was the work of a young artist who had given it to her when he left for Germany. "He did not care to take it with him," she said, and then, seeing me smile, added:"Ah! wait until you have been in the desert for a year, and then come back and look at it again."

It did not need anything like a year, however, for me to become convinced that the artist was right. What, exactly, brought about the change I do not know, but perhaps it was only the natural outcome of existence in a country wherein was no living thing save yourself and your fellows, and the men whom you desired to kill, and who desired to kill you; where was neither beast nor bird, nor any sound save the great soundful silence of the winds, the still music that could be heard sometimes in the purple and scarlet of dawn and dusk, and in the shimmering fury of white-hot noon.

At Luderitzbucht there is a devil-inspired mirage, which day by day paints across the sky a wonder picture of the sea. When first I saw it I sat down on the sand and thought quickly. Then I said to myself: "How funny!. . . but of course it isn't! How could it be?" Then I looked again, and was not quite so sure. The word "mirage" rose glibly enough to my lips, it is true, but did anything that I had ever heard or read of mirages justify it? I asked the question of myself quite seriously.

Mirages are not common objects at home, and most of our knowledge concerning them had been gleaned from the fiction of a past generation. We had even vaguely understood of them that they were a species of "visitation" which manifested themselves only to people who were dying of thirst, and then only in the form of oases or other places where one could obtain drinks. We might have supposed, indeed, that they went out of fashion when drinking, as a pastime, came in. A mirage representing an American cocktail bar would certainly be a tough nut for mere imagination to crack, and, anyway, I was not dying of thirst, or, even if I nearly was, the sea didn't tempt me, so that it did not prove very much either way.

A still, glassy sea it was, marbled with shoal-water, and staked with rocks, and edged with a coquettish display of white foam, but in the endeavour to convey to others something of its impression upon my own mind I confess I find a difficulty in avoiding too lavish a use of the coloured phrase. As a matter of cold, sober fact—if there can be any sobriety at all in such a recollection—there was nothing clear-cut about this amazing sky-picture. Its horizon was all vague and formless—just such a horizon as one may see when looking at a real ocean on one of those days of muffled sunlight, when sky and water seem merged together in a shimmer of grey light. Its foam-faced rocks were a-haze with heat and distance, and at times there would grow upon the wide canvas dark patches that might have been caused by a sudden wind upon the make-believe waters, or—might not.

At Luderitzbucht itself the mirage was only occasionally, and then only very faintly, visible, but at Kolmanskuppe, some nine miles inland, it was almost a permanent feature of the landscape, and I have known men of the infantry regiments stationed there so lost to all sense of proportion and the fitness of things as nearly to come to blows over the hotly debated question of the apparition's *status quo;* and I know of one man, at least, who staked a whole month's pay upon his conviction that it was the sea, and not any trick of desert-magic or chicanery of cloud, as his fellows asserted.

That the changed psychology of men who have been in the desert for a month or so is partly due to actual affection of the eyesight I have little doubt. No man, surely, may spend any length of time in the blind, white glare of those desert-belts, where each morning finds him staring through sand-encrusted eyes at a colour-drunken dawn, and where, at noon, the high hills dance together in the flickering heat haze, and the flat lands quiver and swim across tortured sight, without, eventually, "seeing things," and, what is infinitely worse, believing in them.

Not every day was altogether bad, however. I have known as much as a whole week pass without a sandstorm really worthy of the name, and there were rare days, too, when a soft wind would blow up from the sea and with it a kindly old sea-mist which would help us to endure.

November the 14th will for ever remain a day memorable in the chequered annals of "D" Squadron.

At sunrise, or shortly after, we were disturbed from our usual contemplation of the sand about us by the sound of a motor engine throbbing on the still air. Around us the desert looked rather more illimitable than usual, and as bare of motor traffic as of icebergs. The east was afire with early sunlight, and out of it the deep drone of the engine beat down upon us in solid waves of sound. Louder, louder—a shadow dropped upon us from the skies, and fled away down the sands, and—"Look!" said a man suddenly, "there's an aeroplane!" He spoke in the conversational tone of one who would say, "Look! there's

177

a rainbow!" and we all, as casually as one who would reply, "So there is!" turned and peered in the direction indicated by his outstretched hand. Why, at this point, we felt no particular surprise, nor sensed the faintest premonition of what was coming to us, I shall never know. A dark blur swam slowly across the sun's path; slowly, slowly—ah! The sudden murmur of voices sounded underneath the engine's clatter, and the Taube, with wings atilt, stood out in clear relief against the blue flame of the sky. A confused murmur of interest broke from the watching groups: "By Jove! doesn't it look fine?" "Scouting, I suppose," "Wish I was up there."

The Taube was turning in our direction. It tilted a little more steeply, hung so for a brief instant, and then the planes levelled themselves; there was a quiver or two, and some little rocking—as of a seagull balancing to a headwind—the powerful exhaust of the engine roared down the still air, and—"Look out! he's dropping bombs!" someone shouted. Instinct, rather than sense of ourselves, scattered us like leaves before the wind. There was a sound above us like the savage cracking noise that is sometimes heard in the heart of thunder—a giant stuttering in wrath—and a sense of things dropping swiftly. There followed an instant when the sky fell upon us with a crushing weight of utter silence, and the earth held its breath. Then—the explosion was very near, remember—the firmaments shouted aloud in a thunderclap of sound; and the four dimensions danced drunkenly together, and all that we saw, we who lay where we had flung ourselves upon the sand, or who ran, not knowing why, nor whither, was a feather-headed tower of dust that stood up and bowed gravely to us before it began to droop and drift away.

It is no easy thing, this piecing together of the fragments of memory wherewith to make a story—fragments of things seen swiftly, and, as it were, in a haze, and of things felt, for the most part, subconsciously. He who would paint such a picture must, above all, be honest with himself, and must remember, too, that he cannot attempt to retain on paper that dignity which he has cast utterly away in the sands.

From the middle of November onwards the aeroplane became a more or less regular feature of our lives, and by its aid we were enabled to reduce our weather forecasts to within the limits of an epigram: *"If it blows—hell! if it doesn't—bombs!"* Strangely enough, we preferred it not to blow.

Thirty seconds of bomb-dodging, we argued, was better anyway than twelve hours of burrowing in sand to escape sand, and besides, once the panicky novelty of the Taube had worn off we found more of humour in its visits, and less of that empty feeling at the pit of the stomach which—as you apply it to yourself or to others—is called variously "excitement" and "fear."

For instance, neither excitement nor fear were present, but only laughter, choking and helpless, when, some weeks later, the airman disturbed us at Divine Service in the sands.

From the beginning of things we had always regarded that Sunday morning service as something of an imposition. In a country where there was no visible temptation, this *al fresco* salvation seemed to us a distinct waste of good leisure time, and we barely, listened to the droning voice exhorting us in terms of the Old Testament to soul-heroics as forceful as out of date. Now and again some one in the neighbourhood of the pulpit—a colour-sergeant looking for promotion in both worlds, probably—would chant through his nose the opening bars of a hymn, and we would rise and shuffle our feet until the noise ceased and we could sit down again.

At what period of the service, whether before or after the *De Profundis*, the interruption came, I am at a loss to say. I know that upon one moment I was looking at the ragged toe-caps of my boots and wondering how long they, would last, and upon the next I was on my feet shouting into a chorus of hundreds: "Aeroplane! aeroplane!"

It was a biplane this time, and it was travelling at an immense speed towards us. There was no mistaking its objective. The hundreds of us massed together in one spot must have presented too tempting a mark, and the roar of its engine grew in our ears almost faster than our minds grasped the fact that Divine Service, for the day at least was ended.

But was it? We still stood in something of the congregational order in which we had been paraded earlier on that morning, and there, on the impromptu pulpit, and looking like a black exclamation mark against the pale sky, still remained the surpliced figure which had held all but our attention for the full hour past. The form of subjugation to herd-principles which is known as "discipline" held us rooted to the spot. What would the *padre* do? We were under orders. He was the most tangible expression of those orders in sight, and we watched him as sheep may watch the old bell-wether of the flock.

Our suspense was soon over. Twice the *padre* craned his neck and looked upwards at the 'plane, now circling almost directly, overhead, and twice he looked down at the book in his hand. To me, watching, it

179

seemed that he was debating in his mind some question of comparative values, which, taking everything into consideration, he might very well have been doing. One more upward glance he gave, and then, with an almost indescribably feminine grace of action, swept up the skirts of his surplice, and—there is no other expression for it—bolted like a rabbit.

The fact that no one was killed, or even injured, by the bombs that followed was completely lost sight of in the helpless laughter that held us at intervals throughout the remainder of that memorable Sunday.

What remains to be said of a campaign in which bombs during Divine Service made us laugh, and whereby those who took part gained nothing but an imperishable memory of thirst, and a robust and practical philosophy of the sort that made the Irishman whom I have quoted earlier in this record "*praise the Saints thim ants have no bones into thim!*"

Listen to a group of us talking—I speak not of myself, of course, for I have talked much in these pages—and between the adjectives you will hear much of quaint trifles that do not, properly speaking, belong to war, and very little of the grim things that do.

A page of photographs, taken at random from almost any English weekly paper, will hold more of real war than the combined experiences of all of us could show, and therein, as you may guess, lies the key to our reticence.

You cannot photograph discomfort, or a sandstorm, or thirst, any more than you can photograph humour.

Ah! if you could, you would understand why the curse and the jest are the language of campaigns, and why this faithful narrative must convey a dispiriting sense of much continuously suffered and little occasionally achieved. It is the fault of war: for among the finished operations of war General Botha's drive of the Germans in South West Africa really stands out as brilliantly conceived, swiftly carried out, and emphatically successful.

LEONAUR

ALSO FROM LEONAUR
AVAILABLE IN SOFTCOVER OR HARDCOVER WITH DUST JACKET

THE ART OF WAR by Antoine Henri Jomini—Strategy & Tactics From the Age of Horse & Musket.

THE ART OF WAR by Sun Tzu and Pierre G. T. Beauregard—*The Art of War* by Sun Tzu and *Principles and Maxims of the Art of War* by Pierre G. T. Beauregard.

THE MILITARY RELIGIOUS ORDERS OF THE MIDDLE AGES by F. C. Woodhouse—The Knights Templar, Hospitaller and Others.

THE BENGAL NATIVE ARMY by F. G. Cardew—An Invaluable Reference Resource.

ARTILLERY THROUGH THE AGES—by Albert Manucy—A History of the DEvelopment and Use of Cannons, Mortars, Rockets & Projectiles from Earliest Times to the Nineteenth Century.

THE SWORD OF THE CROWN by Eric W. Sheppard—A History of the British Army to 1914.

THE 7TH (QUEEN'S OWN) HUSSARS: Volume 3—1818-1914 by C. R. B. Barrett—On Campaign During the Canadian Rebellion, the Indian Mutiny, the Sudan, Matabeleland, Mashonaland and the Boer War Volume 3: 1818-1914.

THE CAMPAIGN OF WATERLOO by Antoine Henri Jomini—A Political & Military History from the French perspective.

RIFLE & DRILL by S. Bertram Browne—The Enfield Rifle Musket, 1853 and the Drill of the British Soldier of the Mid-Victorian Period *A Companion to the New Rifle Musket* and *A Practical Guide to Squad and Setting-up Dtill.*

NAPOLEON'S MEN AND METHODS by Alexander L. Kielland—The Rise and Fall of the Emperor and His Men Who Fought by His Side.

THE WOMAN IN BATTLE by Loreta Janeta Velazquez—Soldier, Spy and Secret Service Agent for the Confederancy During the American Civil War.

THE BATTLE OF ORISKANY 1777 by Ellis H. Roberts—The Conflict for the Mowhawk Valley During the American War of Independenc.

PERSONAL RECOLLECTIONS OF JOAN OF ARC by Mark Twain.

CAESAR'S ARMY by Harry Pratt Judson—The Evolution, Composition, Tactics, Equipment & Battles of the Roman Army.

FREDERICK THE GREAT & THE SEVEN YEARS' WAR by F. W. Longman.

9 781782 822387